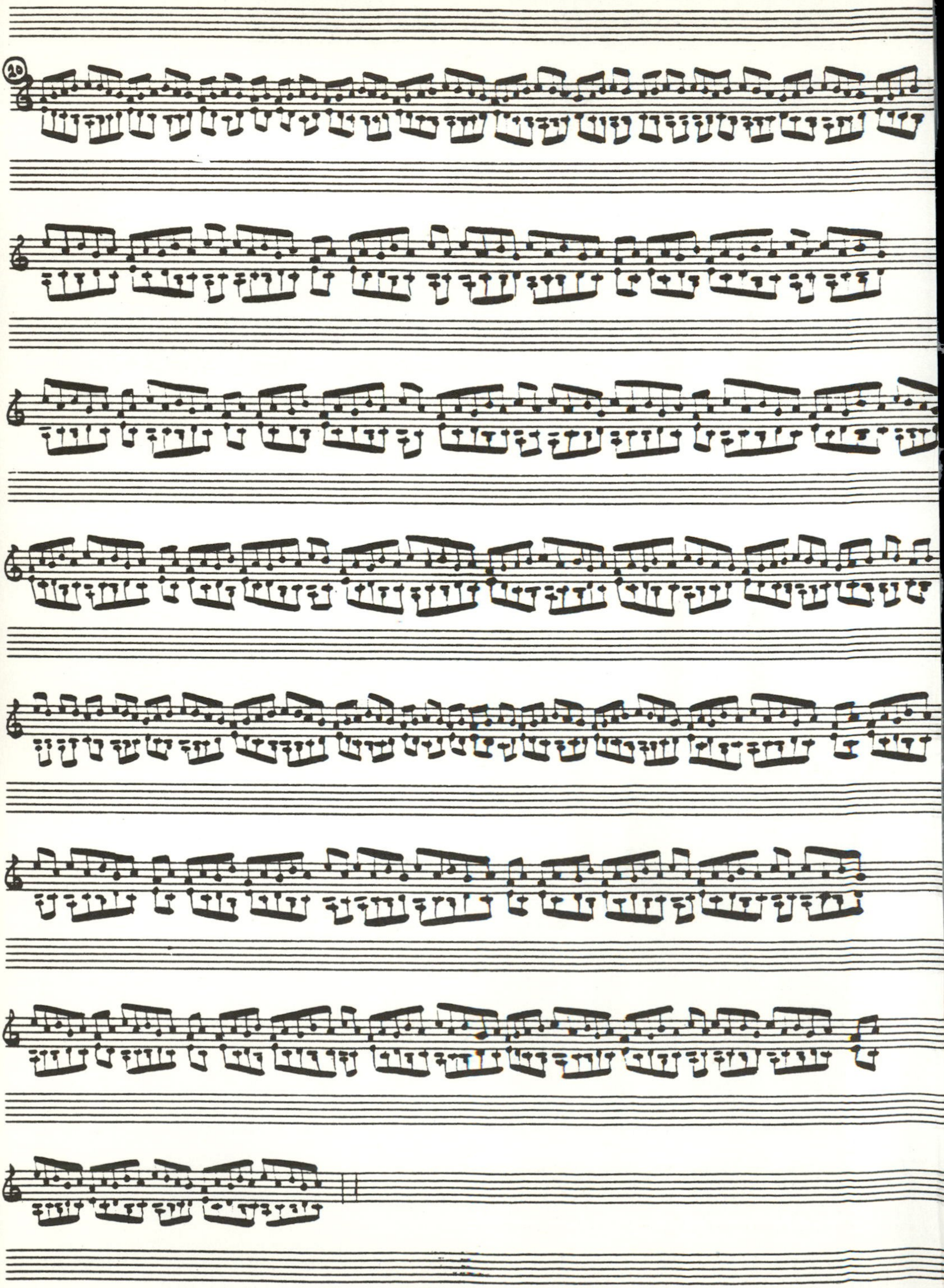
20

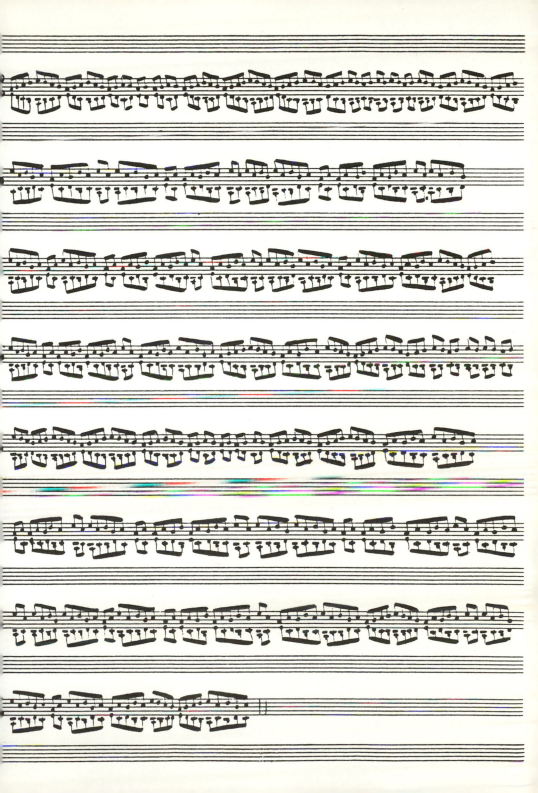

American Minimal Music

To Anne

Wim Mertens

American
Minimal
Music

La Monte Young
Terry Riley
Steve Reich
Philip Glass

Translated by
J Hautekiet
Preface by
Michael Nyman

Kahn & Averill, London
Pro/Am Music Resources Inc., White Plains, NY

First published in Belgium in 1980
First English edition published by Kahn & Averill in 1983

Copyright © 1983 by Wim Mertens

First paperback edition published by Kahn & Averill in 1988

Reprinted in 1991

British Library Cataloguing in Publication Data

Mertens, Wim, *1953 –*
    American minimal music : La Monte Young,
    Terry Riley, Steve Reich, Philip Glass.
    1. Music. Composers – Biographies
    I. Title   II. Amerikanse repetitieve
    muziek. *English*
    780′.92′2

    ISBN 1-871082-00-5

First paperback edition published in the United States in 1988
by Pro/Am Music Resources Inc
White Plains, NY 10606

ISBN 0-912483-15-6

Photoset in 11/12 Plantin

Printed by Halstan & Co. Ltd., Amersham, Bucks., England

Contents

Preface

The four composers whose work provides the basic material for this stimulating and provocative study established their individual and collective musical identities in America in the mid sixties. In 1972 I devoted most of the final chapter of my book *Experimental Music – Cage and Beyond* to these composers: information was somewhat scanty and I was aware of the feeling of breaking dangerous new ground in describing their work in the context of the 'Cage tradition'. At that time Reich's *Drumming* and Glass's *Music with Changing Parts* had just appeared, though Riley's *A Rainbow in Curved Air* had not, and the music was just beginning to break away (as far as one could see from London) from the more or less exclusive following of an admittedly ever-growing circle of initiates. Although one usually has to exempt the work of La Monte Young from any generalised statements about this loosely-connected 'group', the music of at least three of these composers has developed rather startlingly in such a way as to become uniquely accessible to a far more broadly-based audience than seemed possible in 1972: it has been remarkably successful in beginning to break down culturally-erected barriers that separate the 'new music' audience from the 'popular music' audience.

This broadening of appeal (a fascinating dialectic of the music changing the audience and the audience changing the music) can be neatly symbolised both in terms of where the music has been performed in, say, New York (the shift from private lofts and art galleries to the Carnegie Hall and the Bottom Line rock club) and in the way in which it has become (increasingly) available on record (from minority 'new music' classification, poorly-financed art gallery records, self-financed, -produced and -publicised independent labels, to major jazz, rock and classical labels, without any need for classification and categorisation.)

But paradoxically such a quintessentially American and seemingly anti-European music has been largely supported and fostered by European musical institutions: European radio stations, European music festivals, European concert halls and opera houses and in Reich's case, European record companies.

Since 1972 (or even 1974 when *Experimental Music* was published) this music has become something of an established fact and the commentator no longer needs merely to describe or proseletyse: it is now possible, and indeed necessary, to put this music into a broader artistic, cultural, aesthetic, social, musical and critical perspective. Hence the value and relevance of Mertens' book, which approaches this so-called minimal music from a simultaneously broad and detailed viewpoint, is both analytical and polemical, distant and personal, limited to the music itself and yet positioning that music in a wider aesthetic/ideological context than is customary.

Mertens' thesis gains strength from its self-imposed limitations: it deals with the ramifications of the music as music, leaving to other writers the detailed discussion of other cultural cross-connections — with minimal art and structuralist film, with rock and non-Western musical techniques, for example. And Mertens' personal viewpoint gains strength also through its exclusively European orientation: the conceptual, procedural, structural and temporal preoccupations of these composers is not viewed as arising from a radical break with, and separation from recent European musical tradition, but simply as a logical continuation of that tradition. Adorno is invoked as charting the beginning of the breakdown of this tradition in the works of Schoenberg (it is interesting that Adorno's analysis would be far more accurate if for 'Schoenberg' one read 'Cage') and in the works of Deleuze and Lyotard, Mertens has discovered a far more positive and congenial philosophical and ideological context in which to place the music of this earlier but still fruitful generation of American composers.

Michael Nyman
London

1 American Minimal Music

By the designations *American Minimal Music* or "Repetitive Music" one usually understands the music of the composers La Monte Young, Terry Riley, Steve Reich and Philip Glass. These four American composers were the first to apply consistently the techniques of repetition and minimalism in their works. Their music developed in the 1960s in America, and during the seventies became very successful in Europe as well. At the same time the American music seems to have influenced or inspired a great number of European composers, although the nature of this influence and the identity of this European repetitive music is not the subject of this book. It is sufficient to indicate that composers like Michael Nyman and Gavin Bryars in Great Britain, the Dutchman Louis Andriessen, Richard Pinhas and the group Urban Sax in France, Peter Michael Hamel and Michael Fahres in Germany, and the Belgians Karel Goeyvaerts, Frans Geysen and Dominique Lawalrée are implicitly or explicitly concerned with forms of repetition or minimalism in (parts of) their work. Although these composers generally use analogous techniques, they do not share the repetitive aesthetics of the four American composers. Similarly in German *space-rock* of Klaus Schulze or Kraftwerk for instance or in the experimental rock of the (early) XTC or Public Image Ltd (PIL), one can also observe the influence of repetitive music.

Thus we can see a general trend for which the title *minimal music* is only an approximate description. Indeed there are other names in circulation like *repetitive music, acoustical art* and *meditative music* which attempt to pigeonhole this music.

The term *minimal music* refers to the extreme reduction of the musical means the four American composers we are here concerned with use in their works. Obvious though this reduction is, one must ask whether it is important enough to function as a fundamental characteristic of this music. Strictly speaking the term *minimal* can only be applied to the limited initial material and the limited transformational techniques the composers employ, and even this is only the case in the earlier works of Reich and Glass. Certainly one can usually observe in this music a dominant equality of timbre and rhythm, a constant density and a very limited number of pitches. But in terms of length these compositions are certainly not minimal. Terry Riley, for instance, is well known for his *All-Night-Concerts* and Glass's *Music in Twelve Parts* lasts longer than four hours. Moreover, one can see an increase in the rhythmic and harmonic complexity of repetitive music as each of the composers themselves (apart from Young) has developed. While Reich used only six pitches in *Piano Phase* (1967), this number increases to nine in *Music for Mallet Instruments, Voices and Organ* of 1973. And just like Glass, Reich expanded his originally limited and uniform instrumentation, resulting in increasingly differentiated timbres. In *Phase Patterns* (1970), Reich introduces a second (melodic) motive while some ten motives appear in *Drumming* (1971). Thus the term *minimal music* is only partially satisfactory as a label for this tendency.

Moreover, *minimalism* is not the exclusive property of this American music, since one finds "minimal" means are just as much a characteristic of Indian, Balinese and West African music. In fact ethnic music has itself had a strong influence on the works of these four American composers: for Young, Riley and Glass the influence was that of Indian music, while Reich has been influenced by West African and Balinese music.

1 Hatsyiatsya Patterns - Gahu. Ewe-stam (Ghana)

Repetition is also a basic characteristic of European polyphonic music of the Renaissance period finding its most eloquent expression in the so-called 'syntactic style' of structural imitation.

Repetition also features in the decorative (as opposed to structural) imitation of earlier French and Italian secular and sacred music of the 14th century. In the manuscripts *TuB* (c 1400) and *Codex Ivrea* (c 1360) one can find repetition used to illustrate the concept of composition which strives for *le jeu avec le son*. A remarkable example is *Cum Martelli*, an Italian ballad for three voices, in which a scale rising from the tonic to the leading note is gradually built up in the upper voice, and is then broken up in the same manner.

2 An example of repetition in the Italian ballad for three voices, *(Cum Martelli)*

In the *Ars Nova*, the most notable use of repetition is to be found in the *isorhythmic* technique, where fixed melodic and rhythmic series are repeated, usually out of synchronisation. Without attempting to give an exhaustive summary of the use of repetition in European music, a final mention should be made of *Vexations* by Erik Satie, in which the same motive is repeated 840 times, producing a composition that lasts something more than eighteen hours.

In addition to the term *minimal music*, there is also *acoustical art* (Ac' art), which Herman Sabbe has used by analogy with Op Art: "...while the technique of repetition and multiplication of similar short cells, linked in a continuous, *gradually* variegated progression and transition of one motive to another related motive, produces a static, though incessantly moving, acoustic texture, that seems to be an aural analogy to the visual experience of observing an Op Art painting...". This definition does indeed say something about the composition technique employed — the use of identical or similar short cells, the importance of repetition, etc. — as it does also about the psycho-acoustic effects of this music — to produce an acoustic texture and experience that does seem analogous to the visual experience of viewing an op art painting.

And certainly La Monte Young's music undoubtedly parallels in sound the treatment of colour by certain American painters like Newman, Kelly and Noland, whose works confront the retina with vast colour areas that produce unexpected vibrations that appear to pulsate. On the other hand, one has certain reservations as to whether the repetitive use of short cells is the most important compositional technique used by these composers.

If it can be used at all, the term *acoustical art* only applies to Glass's and Reich's music. Glass is not afraid to introduce sudden, unprepared transitions beside the gradual transitions in his music from *Music with Changing Parts* of 1970 onwards. An essential element in his musical thinking is the disorientation of the listener by upsetting, in a treacherous or brutal way, what could seem, at first sight, a music made stable or harmless by the comfort of repetition.

Steve Reich's development has been similar from *Six Pianos* (1973) on, especially in *Music for Mallet Instruments, Voices and Organ* (1973), with its use of sudden transitions in keys or measures. These sudden transitions do not fit the description of the term *ac' art*. In fact, the term is exclusively and entirely applicable only to the music of Terry Riley.

The term *meditative* music too strictly refers to an extra-musical event and stresses that in American music a particular effect on the listener is sought after. Indeed this may be correct, but it is too strong a devaluation of the music to suggest that it is merely a psychological instrument of influence.

The term *repetitive* music — which is also retained in this book — refers to the decisive nature of the repetition as a structural principle in contemporary American music, because this music repeats everything that can be repeated. In its early days the repetition concerned only short or long melodic and rhythmic cells, but later on it was also applied to chord progressions.

The term *repetition*, however, can hardly be used for La Monte Young's music, since in this case the principle of continuity is decisive. However, Young did compose some repetitive works — mainly in his immediate post-Fluxus period — as in his *X for Henry Flynt*. On the other hand, we also find a striving for continuity alongside repetition in the work of Reich and the other composers. Glass, for instance, produces continuity by repeating complexly structured patterns. In the works of Riley, Glass and Reich the use of repetition results in the continuity of the uninterrupted process. This repetition only applies to the micro-structure of their music — the macro-structure is only transformative. Young's approach to repetition is not transformative, and is thus distinguished from the other three composers. Indeed, Young's use of continuity can be considered as a particular form of repetition, so that it is misleading to speak of an opposition between him and the three other composers: there is, at most, a difference in stress.

Before sketching the portraits of these four composers, it might be useful to consider the difference between the use of repetition or techniques of repetition in traditional Western music and American repetitive music.

The use of repetition is not new at all. What is new is only the global musical *context* in which it is used, and it is only this situation that allows us to distinguish between American repetition and repetition in classical music. In traditional music, repetition is used in a pre-eminently *narrative* and *teleological* frame*, so that musical com-

---

* The term *teleology* has its origin in the Greek *telos* (purpose) and originally was a concept in natural philosophy referring to certain directednesses that can be distinguished in nature, and mainly in living nature. Within the modern science of nature a distinction is made between teleology and finality. With teleology, the

ponents like rhythm, melody, harmony and so on are used in a causal, pre-figured way, so that a musical perspective emerges that gives the listener a non-ambivalent orientation and that attempts to inform him of *meaningful* musical *contents*.

The traditional work is *teleological* or end-orientated, because all musical events result in a directed end or synthesis. The composition appears as a musical product characterized by an organic totality. By the underlying dynamic, dramatising construction, a directionality is created that presumes a *linear memory* in the listener, that forces him or her to follow the linear musical evolution. Repetition in the traditional work appears as a *reference to what has gone before*, so that one has to remember what was forgotten. This demands a learned, serious and concentrated, memory-dominated approach to listening. The music of the American composers of repetitive music can be described as non-narrative and a-teleological. Their music discards the traditional harmonic functional schemes of tension and relaxation and (currently) disapproves of classical formal schemes and the musical narrative that goes with them (formalizing a tonal and/or thematic dialectic). Instead there appears non-directed evolution in which the listener is no longer submitted to the constraint of following the musical evolution.

directedness is defined but one cannot determine scientifically whether there is also an intention behind it. Here the distinction is made between *Zweck* and *Absicht*, *End* and *Purpose*. We will not retain this distinction, except in the sense of external and internal musical purposes. The external musical directedness corresponds to what is above called *Absicht* and *Purpose*. It includes the expression of feelings, the symbolisation of situations and the imitation of actions. In this sense, teleological music is a music that has a representative function. (Programme music is a particular example of this external directedness).

Internal directedness refers to the evolution within the music itself, and not to a representational content directed from the outside. In Western music, this kind of directedness is realized through the strong stress on harmony, which can be seen as an evolutional model aiming at a final climax. Thus, Western music is essentially *dialectical*: development follows from the presence of a conflict between opposites and finally leads to a situation of synthesis, in which conflicts are entirely or partially resolved. This can be called *narrative* by analogy with the evolution of a classical novel, in which the dénouement resolves the conflicts of the plot.

The concepts "teleology" and "narrative" run in parallel so that, as in the case of teleology, a distinction can be made between the narrative in the external and internal sense.

3 La Monte Young, Pandit Pran Nath and Marian Zazeela

The Composers and their works

La Monte Young

La Monte Young was born in Bern, Idaho, on October 14, 1935. At an early age he played guitar, saxophone and clarinet and learned how to tap-dance. In interviews Yound has said that as a boy he was greatly impressed by noises like the incessant whistling of the wind, the humming of insects, running water and the rustling of trees.

Later on he became fascinated by jazz musicians like Lee Konitz, Eric Dolphy and John Coltrane and from 1955 till 1956 Young studied composition with Leonard Stein, a colleague of Arnold Schoenberg. At the University of California, Los Angeles, Young studied music theory, composition, and ethno-musicology. In the summer of 1959, he attended Karlheinz Stockhausen's seminars in Darmstadt and he made an intensive study of John Cage's works. In 1960 Young went to New York to study electronic music with Richard Maxfield, in the 'New School for Social Research' where he also met George Maciunas, the 'leader' of the Fluxus 'movement'. It was only after he had finished this training that Young began to write music. He worked for *Beatitude*, Chester Anderson's magazine which published important scores, poems and texts and which seems to have been a stimulus for Fluxus. The editors of *Beatitude* invited Young to make a special edition that did not appear in its desired form, but which became the foundation of *An Anthology* (1963), which Young put together with Maciunas and Jackson Mac Low. This book was a collection of scores, essays, dance constructions, poetry, concept art, etc., by a number of artists; Earle Brown, Dick Higgins, Christian Wolff, Richard Maxfield and Young himself. It was republished by Heiner Friedrich in Munich in 1970.

With Maciunas and Mac Low, he also set up 'performances' involving Joseph Byrd, Henry Flynt, Richard Maxfield and Toshi

Ichyanagi. As musical director, Young worked for some years for the choreographer Ann Halprin, often in conjunction with Terry Riley. In 1963 he married the painter and light artist Marian Zazeela, with whom he had worked since 1962. And in the same year he formed "The Theatre of Eternal Music" with her, an ensemble which included Tony Conrad, the well-known producer of minimal movies and John Cale, which was devoted solely to the peformance of his own music.

With Zazeela he also compiled *Selected Writings*, a volume of his writings and interviews. From 1970 on Young and Zazeela studied with the Indian musician Pandith Pran Nath. After an intensive period of concert work in Europe in the first half of the seventies, Young has performed less and less in public.

La Monte Young's work can be divided into three periods. From 1956 till 1958 he wrote serial music: between 1959 and 1961 Young's work was part of Fluxus; and it is from 1962 that what one would call his actual repetitive period starts. But there is an extreme continuity between these three periods, and the transition between periods is a gradual process that can be illustrated by the comparison of *Five Small Pieces for String Quartet on remembering a Niad* (1956) and *Octet for Brass*, composed a year later. Both pieces are written in a mainly serial style, but the length of the sustained notes gradually increases. Though long notes already appear in *Five Small Pieces*, Young says he introduced consciously long notes, sometimes lasting three or four minutes — within the serial style — for the first time only in his *Octet*. Young's serial works are clearly precursors of his later compositions in that they favour spare textures with long-held pitches which are very limited in number.

Anton Webern's works interest Young particularly. He was attracted by certain aspects of Webern's music, especially the duality between its structural variation and the static sound that results from it. In Webern there is a tendency to produce continuous variations by using notes in the same octave position throughout a piece, whatever their position in the row. However, the listener perceives this process more as a stasis, as if the same information is being repeated over and over again.

The *String Trio* for violin, viola, and cello, or for string orchestra (1958), the most important work of this period, refines the long-note-style, and results in the elimination of each melodic line in favour of a harmonic consonance and long periods of silence. This way of working is opposed to the one he used in *For Guitar* of the same year, where, taking into account the playing technique of the acoustic guitar, no long-held tones appear but only long notes that last three or four minutes*.

The use of long notes is in itself no novelty, but up till recently they were only used as a drone over which a melody was placed. For Young it is precisely these long notes that are the subject of his music. They do not play the role of an individual part, but they contribute to an overall sound spectrum, as a result of which the components have a different duration. The consonance is far more important than the vertical development of the individual parts. About *Trio* we can say that the timbres are deliberately colourless, and the slowly bowed tones are played without vibrato. The dynamic levels are not constant, but are limited to the range from *pppp* to *p*.

In 1959, Young worked along with Terry Riley for the choreographer Ann Halprin. Together they experimented with very long, unusual sounds that are held for minutes or sometimes hours on end. This method of working, together with the combination of dance and theatre — so important in Fluxus — and the stress on improvisation, point to the direction of Young's later works.

Fluxus is an anti-art movement, a movement of art nihilism and concretism, attempting to create a close, unbreakable link between art and life. The movement has George Maciunas to thank for its name. Maciunas indicated three aspects of Fluxus in a 1963 manifesto: as a revolution realizing the interaction between art and life, regarded purely as a means for releasing excess tension, and as catalyst in the united front of socio-political revolutionaries. The purposes of the movement are, according to Maciunas, more of a social than of an aesthetic nature. Art has to become comprehensible to everybody and he disapproves of art as an object without function, of the artificial separation between artists and audience, of individualism in art, etc... In brief, the purposes can be paraphrased under the slogan: "Art is Life, and Life is Art". Fluxus can be considered as the musical equivalent of the 'Happening' in visual arts. Fluxus is more anarchistic

* *For Guitar* (1958) was given its first performance only in December 1979 in The Kitchen, New York, by Ned Sublette.

though, and often expresses itself in aggressive, destructive brutality and in the deliberate irritation of the audience.

Protagonists from all branches of art worked in Fluxus. Among them were George Brecht, Dick Higgins, Ben Vautier, La Monte Young, John Cage, Chieko Shiomi and Nam June Paik.

The start of Young's Fluxus period can be situated in 1959, when he first heard John Cage's music in Darmstadt, more particularly the works Cage wrote after his String Quartet and his *Sonatas and Interludes* for prepared piano: *Concert for Piano and Orchestra* of 1958, played by David Tudor, especially impressed Young. In his *Lecture 1960*, he says that his activities with Ann Halprin were the most decisive in determining the direction of his later works. Through his improvisations with Riley he discovered that people have always tried to force sounds to express what the composer wants, and this produces the kind of boredom he experiences when listening to most traditional music. "We must let sounds be what they are," Young says. Young wants to make it clear that sounds have their own existence, independent of human existence. This approach has an educative aspect: a sound does not have to be linked successively with another sound to be interesting; it is interesting in itself, and only when produced for a very long time can we learn anything from it.

A second important influence in Young's works is the work in electronic music he did in 1960 with Richard Maxfield, musical director in Yoko Ono's studio and very much appreciated by Young as sound engineer and composer. As in Young's work, the stress in Maxfield's music is on static composition and progressive development.

Young still retained his convinced Fluxus attitude and without interruption went in search of new sounds. In 1959-60 Young wrote pieces of a destructive nature and works where instruments are treated in fairly unusual ways, and in which an indeterminate element plays an important part. Examples are *Vision* for eleven instruments (in which numbers in a telephone directory determine the time and space in which the thirteen well-defined sounds are created), *Piano Piece for David Tudor No. 1* and *Composition 1960 No. 2*. He also gives attention to the social aspects of performance, in *Composition 1960 No. 3, No. 4*, and *No. 6* for example.

Piano Piece for David Tudor #1

Bring a bale of hay and a bucket
of water onto the stage for the
piano to eat and drink. The
performer may then feed the piano
or leave it to eat by itself. If the ·
the former, the piece is over after
the piano has been fed. If the
latter, it is over after the piano
eats or decides not to.

October 1960

4 Piano Piece for David Tudor No 1

Composition 1960 #2

Build a fire in front of the audience. Preferably, use wood although other combustibles may be used as necessary for starting
the fire or controlling the kind of smoke. The fire may be of
any size, but it should not be the kind which is associated
with another object, such as a candle or a cigarette lighter.
The lights may be turned out.

After the fire is burning, the builder(s) may sit by and watch
it for the duration of the composition; however, he (they) should
not sit between the fire and the audience in order that its members will be able to see and enjoy the fire.

The composition may be of any duration.

In the event that the performance is broadcast, the microphone
may be brought up close to the fire.

5 · 5 · 60

Composition 1960 #3

Announce to the audience when the piece will begin and end if there is a limit on duration. It may be of any duration.

Then announce that everyone may do whatever he wishes for the duration of the composition.

5 · 14 · 60

Composition 1960 #4

Announce to the audience that the lights will be turned off for the duration of the composition (it may be any length) and tell them when the composition will begin and end.

Turn off all the lights for the announced duration.

When the lights are turned back on, the announcer may tell the audience that their activities have been the composition, although this is not at all necessary.

6 · 3 · 60

Composition 1960 #6

The performers (any number) sit on the stage watching and listening to the audience in the same way the audience usually looks at and listens to performers. If in an auditorium, the performers should be seated in rows on chairs or benches; but if in a bar, for instance, the performers might have tables on stage and be drinking as is the audience.

Optional: A poster in the vicinity of the stage
reading: COMPOSITION 1960 #6
by
La Monte Young
admission

(price)

and tickets, sold at stairways
leading to stage from audience,
admitting members of the audience
who wish to join the performers on
stage and watch the remainder of
the audience.

A performance may be of any duration.

July 2, 1960

5 Composition 1960 Nos 2,3,4 & 6

In *Composition 1960 No. 3* Young asks that the beginning and
ending of the piece be announced, and indicates that during that
time-period there is total freedom of action. In *Composition 1960 No. 4*
the audience does not know when the work starts, how it develops and
when it stops; the lights are turned out and after some time — when
the lights are on again — people are informed that the subject of the
piece was the actions and reactions of the audience. *Composition 1960
No. 6* portrays best of all the traditional rôle of performer and audience
by having the former observe the latter.

In *Two Sounds*, from the middle of his Fluxus period, characteristics
of Young's later work appear again, namely the use of sustained tones
and a long overall duration. The composer sees sound as atomic, as a
singular event isolated from its surroundings. Dieter Schnebel speaks,
in this context, of "through-composed momentary musical snapshots".
Young faithfully follows John Cage's aesthetic since he also wants to
"free sound of all local and physiological ballast". However, a difference between Young and Cage lies in Young's concentration on
only one event, while Cage's works treat different events occurring
simultaneously in a given period of time. Young's Fluxus activities
culminated in the foundation of the "Theatre of the Singular Event".

The first sound of *Two Sounds* is generated by a circular friction of
metal against glass, the second through friction of metal against
wood. Al Hansen wrote in his book about 'happenings' that this

sound was held 15 to 20 minutes; it resembled the grinding of train wheels, and was greated with shouts and catcalls during the first performance.

Characteristic of this music is the use of extremely reduced sound material — only two sounds — and, as will be seen later, the conscious observation of the effect on the listener. "Simultaneously," John Cage remarks, "the attentive listener is struck by the simplicity of the action and by the complexity of the sound". Young's desire is to penetrate the inner essence of the sound, and he has remarked that the only way to do this is to sustain the sound for a long time. And it is significant that *Composition 1960 No. 7* consists of an open 5th with the instruction "to be held for a long time".

6 Composition 1960 No 7

The absence of anarchistic, destructive or aggressive characteristics in a piece like this makes some critics conclude that Young's work is not part of the Fluxus ideal. For others the link with Fluxus exists because the required length of the piece aims only at the irritation of the audience, while others consider this work to be part of a transitory phase to Young's repetitive period.

In 1962 Young wrote *The Second Dream of the High-Tension Line Stepdown Transformer* which marks his switch to electronics. For this he selected four pitches and prescribed which of the four can sound together and which cannot. The notes concerned have the frequency ratios 36-35-32-24. This means that, if we assume that the lowest note is G, the three others sould be C, C ♯ (less than half a tone from D) and D.

The length of the sounds is determined by the performers, but has to be long enough to enable the listener to distinguish gradually the overtones and combination tones. The foundation of this music is the *drone*: continuous, low, sustained sounds, which Young realized initially with a frequency generator but from 1969 on with a Moog synthesizer.

However, at this point Young had not yet made a specific move in the direction of repetitive music. The works of 1961 do point to a number of aspects that are shown in this kind of music. Young keeps concentrating on the singular unique event, and at different points during that year he wrote the same composition 29 times: *Draw a straight line and follow it*. This is the same composition as his *Composition 1960 No. 10* — in fact Young wrote 30 differently dated pieces, with the instruction *Draw a straight line and follow it*. The first composition that employs actual repetition as a structural principle dates from 1960 and is known as *Arabic Numeral (any integer) for Henry Flynt* or *X for Henry Flynt*. It prescribes a heavy sound or cluster being repeated uniformly, regularly and for a long period. The work differs from the music of other composers of repetitive music in repeating one and the same sound and not a motive or succession of differend sounds. The essence of Young's Fluxus-inspired works is to look for a means to let the music explore the world of the sound in an unusual but therefore more efficient way. Young's Fluxus period should be seen as a transition period in which the most important basic characteristics of his work, like held notes and long duration, are further developed.

In 1967, Young formed his own ensemble — The Theatre of Eternal Music. He even considered a space for the permanent performance of his music and thus the "Dream House" project was created in 1964. Young envisaged this "Dream House" as a space in which people live and make music. Initially the ensemble consisted of Young, soprano saxophone; Angus McLise, percussion; Marian Zazeela, voice, and Tony Conrad and John Cale, strings. Almost all the music that Young wrote after 1962, such as *The Tortoise, his Dreams and Journeys*, consists of two levels: one level made up of preselected pitches that are held continuously, as the basis, the subject of the music, and a second level of long-held pitches which form the basis for improvisation. On this second level the pitches are also selected according to which of them are consonant in the improvisation and which are not. Exceptions from this compositional technique are *The Second Dream*,

Studies in the Bowed Disc, and *The Well-Tuned Piano.*

   The Well-Tuned Piano of 1964 is the most frequently played work
from The Theatre of Eternal Music and is still in Young's current
repertoire, along with excerpts from *Tortoise* (see later). The pitches
in *The Well-Tuned Piano* are selected according to the harmonic
relationship between the notes: only those notes that have an overtone
relationship to each other, or both to a third, can be used. The
relationship between the overtone and the key-tone must be reducible
to a simple fraction. Therefore *The Well-Tuned Piano* cannot be
played at a keyboard in tempered tuning, because in that tuning only
a G and an A have a frequency that can be expressed in whole
numbers.

7 La Monte Young: *The Well-Tuned Piano*

   Why then, one could ask, does La Monte Young aim for this
precision? The reason lies in the relationship between periodicity and
repetition. Precisely these harmonic sounds can, because of their
proportional relationship to the key-tone, be expressed in whole
numbers, one periodic and regularly repetitive. This mathematic
precision also has physiological consequences. Daniel Caux says that
"the relationship between two or more frequencies can best be
assumed by the human brain when the information is periodic".
Young becomes increasingly interested in the determination of this
kind of influence on the listener.

Like *The Well-Tuned Piano*, *The Second Dream* is a piece that only consists of one sound line. This also goes for *Studies in the Bowed Disc* (1963), a work in which Young and Zazeela bow a gong specially manufactured for this work by sculptor Robert Morris. Young and Zazeela decide, independently, how long to bow the gong for, resulting in a sustained sound mass. Unlike previous pieces, a noise is produced instead of pitches that are adapted to each other, and another difference lies in the use of improvisation at ground level.

In 1964 the personnel of The Theatre of Eternal Music changed and from 1964 till 1966, it included Young, who no longer played the saxophone but sang instead; Zazeela, voice; Conrad and Cale, strings and (sometimes) Terry Riley, voice.

The new line-up coincides with the beginning of performances of *The Tortoise, His Dreams and Journeys*, and from 1965 on Marian Zazeela's light-environment *The Ornamental Lightyears Tracery*, is an integral part of The Theatre of Eternal Music performances. And just as Young carefully selects pitches and adapts them to each other, Zazeela groups slides that belong to each other. The intensity of the "light bundles", the purity of the colours and the effect of one colour on another are often adapted to the musical event.

The Second Dream is a direct precursor of *The Tortoise*. The tortoise acts as metaphor for the idea of playing the piece continuously — a piece which has no beginning or end and which thus cannot be recognised as a limited whole. Young's performances are meant to be excerpts of the total work that is supposed to continue between performances, which themselves only take up the interrupted thread. *The Tortoise* music is modal; Young still uses basic pitches, the drones that are sustained for an unlimited period of time. Young says of these drones that "they are the first sound in the Tortoise's life. They are primitive sounds that do not remember ever to have started and that are perpetuated in the Dream House project". The preselected drones serve as the starting point for an improvisation in which the overtones are strictly adapted to this key-note. Thus simple intervals are created in which the continuity of the drone is central and overtones are added only to obtain more relief. From the consonance of key-note and overtones spring combination tones, the so-called sum and difference tones, which finally results in a very complex sound. "We do not necessarily experience frequencies as a consequence or as a melody, they can as well be observed as a proportion to a fixed tone", says Young.

In *Drift Studies* (1966), Young experiments with harmonically adapted sine tones, and is part of the total *Tortoise* project: they are studies in the deviation effects that are created when simultaneous oscillation produces two or more constant sine waves. These deviation effects are caused by a change in the phase relation of the sine waves which, despite the high stability of the oscillators, deviate in pitch. One gets the "sensational feeling that the body softly starts flowing off in space and time synchronously with these waves", says Young.

A second effect of *Drift Studies* has to do with the division of the air pressure areas in a room. In the high pressure areas the sound is louder than in low pressure areas. For Young the positioning and the spatial mobility of the listener are an integral part of the experience of the composition. From 1966 on Young always used electronically generated frequencies to produce his continuous sounds, whereas previously the drones had been produced by an audio-frequency generator tuned to a certain pitch, or by a turtle-motor that had previously been used to run an aquarium filter. But from the end of the sixties Young produced his drones by means of the ultra stable sine wave oscillators of a Moog synthesizer built especially for Young's work. In 1966 he composed *Map of 49's dream the two systems of eleven sets of galactic intervals Ornamental Lightyears Tracery*. This total environment, part of the *Tortoise, his Dreams and Journeys*, consists of a series of light and sound frequencies whose basis is *The Two systems of eleven categories 1:07:40 AM 3X 67*– an adaptation of *2–3 PM i2 X1 66–3: 43: AM 28X11 66 for John Cage from Vertical Hearing in the Present Tense*. *Vertical Hearing in the Present Tense* is a theoretical work dealing with the total dominance of the harmonic structure of the music, in which Young describes a method of controlling, with acute precision, the combined and the generated frequences. (*Generated* frequencies are tones produced by the voice, a musical instrument or an oscillator and *combined* frequencies are the sum and difference tones that are produced when two or more generated frequencies sound together).

Map of 49's Dream also examines the effect of continuous, periodic sound waves on an audience exposed to these sounds for a number of hours. By this means Young realised one of his main purposes, namely the creation of a totally surrounding environment made up of frequency structures in sound and light. The first public performance of this show was given in 1969 in the Heiner Friedrich gallery in Munich.

Since 1966 Young has had a sound-producing installation in his

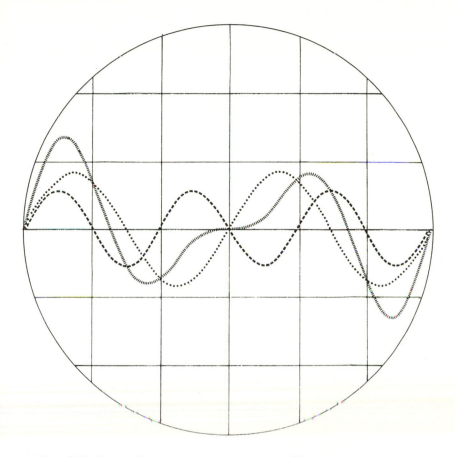

8 *Map of 49's Dream*: the two systems of eleven sets of Galactic intervals ornamental Light-years Tracery

house in New York. These systems are audible for 24 hours a day, and sometimes last for weeks or months. He and Marian Zazeela work and live in this space and frequently invite people who are asked to inform them of their reactions, and these are later made the subject of extensive reports.

In order to master the precise intonation required in the vocal parts in *Map of 49's Dream*, Young and Zazeela have studied with Pandit

Pran Nath, whose Indian musical training has given him a very strong control over vocal pitch. Young says that it is hard to pitch sine tones without their overtones, and that often too much importance is attached to melody: "Melody does not exist at all (The Disappearance of Melody), unless one is forced to hear as melodic the movement of a group of different simultaneously sounding frequencies, deduced from one series of overtones to another, due to previous musical conditioning. Even before the first human being went from one frequency to another (melody), the relationship of the second frequency to the first was predetermined (harmonically) by the overtone-structure of the key-tone of the first tone. And in the Tortoise's life, the drone is the first tone."

Terry Riley

Terry Riley was born in Colfax, California, on June 24, 1935. From 1955 till 1957 he studied composition at the San Francisco State College. Later he worked under Robert Erickson, studied piano with Duane Hampton at the San Francisco Conservatoire of Music with Adolf Baller. He financed his studies by working as a ragtime pianist in the Gold Street Saloon in San Francisco. Riley wrote his first composition at the age of 19. He formed an improvisation group with Pauline Oliveros and Loren Rush and during 1959 and 1960 he and La Monte Young worked with choreographer Ann Halprin. He finished his studies at the University of California, Berkeley, in 1961 with Seymour Shifrin and William Denny. For two years from 1962, Riley toured around Europe. In France he performed with a theatre company and in Scandinavia he took part in 'happenings', street theatre and jazz-concerts. At this time Riley gave his first All-Night-Concerts, playing saxophone and several keyboard instruments, and when he also began composing his first repetitive works. Back in New York in 1964 Riley began to examine the possibilities of electro-acoustic music.

In 1967, the Royal Academy of Music of Stockholm and the Swedish Radio invited him to produce musical programmes and give lectures. In the same year he gave an All-Night-Concert in the Philadelphia College of Art where *An All Night Flight* for solo-saxophone lasting 8 hours and 30 minutes was first performed.

During this period, Riley often worked with Arlo Acton, who devised spherical loudspeakers to give optimal sound reproduction. In 1969 Riley received an award for the music he composed for the film *Music with Balls*. Like La Monte Young and Marian Zazeela, Terry Riley has also been a pupil of Pandit Pran Nath.

Riley's music has influenced a number of American and European avant-garde composers and many jazz and pop musicians. The Soft Machine's *Moon in June* is a clear example of this — in fact, the co-founder of this group, David Allen, was a good friend of Riley's. The English group Third Ear Band also show their debt to Riley in their use of "modal patterns on the principle of periodic progression".

With John Cale, Riley recorded the LP *Church of Antrax* and the Berlin-based band Agitation Free included his *In C* in its repertoire. And, finally, the pop group Curved Air took its name from Riley's *A Rainbow in Curved Air*.

While La Monte Young's early compositions were influenced by Schoenberg, Terry Riley was initially influenced by Stockhausen. For *Spectra*, a piece with different tempo levels for six instruments, written during his youth, Riley was awarded the Nicola di Lorenzo prize; although it evidently borrows from Stockhausen's *Zeitmasse* for five wind instruments, Riley's modal way of writing is quite remarkable. The *String Quartet* of the same period is closer to classical Western music.

During 1959 and 1960, Riley's and La Monte Young's improvisations, which gave their great scope for experiment and accident, served as accompaniment to Ann Halprin's dance. Although they used unconventional means of producing sounds they did not use non-electronic sound source. Around the same period, Cage's influence on their work becomes more and more obvious through the interest they show in acoustic phenomena as such. In 1960, after their experiments with Ann Halprin, Riley wrote an untitled work for two pianos and made various tapes, still showing the influence of Stockhausen. Though both Young and Riley were interested in the physiological and psychical effects of music, they both had very different attitudes to these effects. Riley's music develops out of a marginal aspect of Young's work, namely the repetition that Young used in *Arabic Numeral (any integer) for Henry Flynt* and *Dorian Blues*. While La Monte Young considers repetition as a controlling mechanism, Riley sees repetition more as a means of forming his unusual material.

This shows a number of differences between the music of both composers. Riley replaces the constant in Young's work with continuously-evolving repetition and multiplication techniques. A short motive or sound cell is repeated until the performer decides it should be changed or replaced. The different cells in such compositions or improvisations are very closely related to each other. For Riley, repetition in itself has no purpose other than being a musical means to "rouse emotional vibrations in the listener". Indeed Riley has said that he would have been willing to drop repetition immediately if another system could have brought him closer to his purpose.

And while Young increasingly restricted compositional freedom, improvisation assumed an ever more important role with Riley. Initially he wrote the musical cells in traditional notation and in pieces left it for the performers to determine the number of repetitions of each cell. But later on Riley restricted his activities to solo concerts in which improvisation becomes increasingly important.

Riley used two multiplication systems in his solo work: *tape-loop*, a looped length of tape that repeats the same figure continuously, and *tape-delay*, a method that served as an electronic quasi-feedback system. Riley used tape loops for the first time in his tape piece *The Five Legged Stool* in 1961, and used feedback for the first time in the 1963 soundtrack for Ken Devey's *The Gift*. For this production he collaborated with the trumpeter Chet Baker and his jazz quintet. Pre-recorded tapes of the group were played back by the sound engineer with slow echo and were repeated through a feedback system which built the sounds up in cycles. This was a crucial discovery for Riley's succeeding projects, in which the idea of a cyclic structure frequently occurs. In *Dorian Reeds* the tape delay technique was used for the first time. This is a procedure by which a given motive is played by an instrument recorded and reproduced with a short delay which is brought about by the relative positions of the recording and replay heads of the tape machines. A second tape recorder can be used and placed some feet away from the first so that the original material can be heard a third time. *Dorian Reeds* includes a number of elements such as its instrumentation and the use of basic motifs which he developed further in *Keyboard Studies* and *In C*. Composed in the Dorian mode, *Dorian Reeds* can also be named *Dorian Winds*, *Dorian Voices*, and so on, depending on which instruments are used in a particular performance. The basic figure of the piece consists of the

series C G F♯ G F♯C A, which is repeated throughout, though ad-
ditional motifs vary this series rhytmically and melodically.

In *Keyboard Studies No. 2* (1964), Riley used a series of fifteen
modal figures each of which revolve around two or four notes of the
mode. The first figure is repeated continuously as a background
pulse, against which other figures are outlined. By means of this
repetition, each figure acquires its own rhythmic and melodic profile.
The vertical combination of sounds is relatively unimportant, since
what is important is the superposition of lines and not a succession of
vertical combinations. At this point, Riley's melodic/rhythmic music
can again be set against Young's music with its almost exclusive
emphasis on harmony. Because the performers have the freedom to
create several new patterns (which Steve Reich, in reference to his
own music later called *resulting patterns*), the result sounds entirely
different from what can be deduced from the score.

10 Keyboard Studies No 2

In *Keyboard Studies No. 2* only eight different notes are used, though octave doublings make the number up to twelve, spanning only an octave and a fourth. Overall duration is not determined, and the length of the separate sounds may be long or short, provided they are of equal length. Changes in dynamics are not permitted and all parts have to be performed at an identical volume, namely *forte*. None of the individual figures is given any more importance than any of the others and all notes are struck with equal, even attacks. Riley notates the fifteen melodic cells in the traditional way, adding infinity signs to indicate the high number of repetitions required.

The motives develop out of one another. The third figure, for instance, is an extension of the second, which itself repeats notes of the first figure in a different order; the last three notes of the fourth figure are the same as the third; the tenth figure is an inversion of the second, and so on. The first cell is the basic figure in two respects: it is both a continuous base figure and a generator of all the other figures.

Many of the *Keyboard Studies* series were not written down, because of the emphasis on improvisation. The name *Keyboard Studies* is appropriate because Riley literally considered these pieces or improvisations as daily exercises to be used as preparation for his solo concerts.

Many of the series of pieces — they were never presented as *works* — are not dated, or if they are, only vaguely. *Keyboard Studies No. 2* (or *The Untitled Organ*) is dated 1966 in John Cage's *Notations*, but according to Daniel Caux it was written in 1964. Another study in the series, *Keyboard Studies No. 7* (1967) clearly illustrates through its notation the cyclic design that we find in many of Riley's compositions.

Three figures are written out on seven concentric circular staves. The figure on the outside stave is the simplest and only includes four notes: G, Bb, F, Ab, from which the other figures are deduced. The next five circles carry the same figure, but are arranged according to superimposed phase shifts. Thus we find the extended first figure:

...	g'	ab'	g'	bb'	f'	bb'	ab	...		
	...	g'	ab'	g'	bb'	f'	bb'	ab'	...	
		...	g'	ab'	g'	bb'	f'	bb'	ab'	...
...	g'	ab'	g'	bb'	f'	bb'	ab'	...		
...	...	g'	ab'	g'	bb'	f'	bb'	ab'	...	

The middle circle has one more pitch: the seven-note theme of the previous parts, extended with a high C. All circles have the same number of notes, namely 56.

11 Keyboard Studies No 7 (1967)

To sum up, we can say that Riley's works are made up of cells that are continuously repeated and produce ever-new combinations. Thus his music is produced by the superimposition of a number of individual lines which the listener observes in ever-different ways through repetition and overlapping of predictable accents. It is characteristic of this evolving repetition that a dualism gradually emerges between the micro-structure of the sounds and the macro-structure of the composition. The constant change at micro-level is indeed linked to the texture that remains largely invariable and static. Hence the suggestion of immobility that Riley's music gives after some time, despite the quick tempi. Thus Tim Souster's opinion that "with Riley it is not what happens at each moment that is important, but what counts is the development of the whole time process".

In 1964, Riley composed *In C* which is generally considered as the typical pulse piece, though a pulse was implicit in the regularity of the repeating figures in *Keyboard Studies No. 2* and *Dorian Reeds*. *In C*, on the other hand, is considerably more complex, since there are 53 different figures offering far more rhythmic and melodic variation than does *Keyboard Studies*. The composition develops from the idea of starting *loops* of different lengths on different tape-recorders bringing about a constant network of overlappings. All the parts are regulated by and refer to, the pulse of a continuously repeated high quaver C. Every part is of equal importance, there is no accompanied melody and no foreground or background. All performers play from the same score but they may start at different times and choose the number of repetitions for themselves. This means that each player will take a different length of time to run through the cells. The type and number of instruments are free, the only limitation being that only instruments capable of playing the prescribed pitches may be used. Unlike *Keyboard Studies*, which can be performed as a solo piece, *In C* is genuinely and exclusively an ensemble piece.

12 Thirty-five of the fifty-three figures from *In C* (1964)

An important feature of *In C* is the limited improvisational freedom it gives to the performers. Riley almost exclusively concentrates on the definition of form that "has to be simple enough to lead the improvisational ensemble of the musicians through good channels". Nobody is allowed to play as a soloist, but at the same time, even though the form has to be respected, this does not hinder the performer's free expression.

From 1967 on, Riley appeared more and more frequently as soloist/improvisor in a series of so-called *All-Night-Concerts*. For Riley's music — whose intention was to rouse the listener's emotional vibrations — it was necessary to place a large number of loudspeakers around the audience. "The music has to flow in our bloodstream and we have to be carried by its bloodstream", Riley has said.

A Rainbow in Curved Air was composed in 1967 for electronic organ and clavichord, rocksichord, tambourine and dumbec, all played by Riley using every technique of *overdubbing*. At the base of this composition lies a theme of fourteen notes, consisting of two figures played by the left hand.

13 Basic left-hand figure from *A Rainbow in Curved Air* (1967)

The first figure consists of two cells of three notes, the second is a variant of this consisting of two cells of four notes. The figures and cells can be combined with each other, though the order within the cells has to be respected. The melodic evolution of the theme allows each note to be the beginning or end of a musical phrase. This retrograde theme runs through the piece as a *loop-part*. A definite tonality is nowhere established. Two plateaus can be distinguished during the course of the piece, the first being a pure repetition (or pulse) plateau, the second being built up improvisationally.

In *Persian Surgery Dervishes* (1970-1971) Riley elaborates one of his favourite figures, namely A G A♭ B♭ F, which appears in his works from 1964 onwards. His first improvisations *Autumn Heavers* and *Untitled Organ* (or *Keyboard Studies No. 2*) use it and it also appeared in *Keyboard Studies No. 7*. Except for this one written theme, one can hardly speak of a score in *Persian Surgery Dervishes*. Riley considers the function of notation in general to be more like an aide-mémoire.

It is precisely in the freedom that Riley gives to his performers (for example, *In C* or the subsequent *Olson III* of 1967 for instrumental ensemble and childrens' choir) that he differs most obviously from Young, Reich and Glass, who write music that is much more strictly organized. First of all Riley is a performer who composes and not a composer in the narrow sense of the word. As with other composers of repetitive music one can observe in Riley's music an increasing complexity over the years, which in his case results from his increasing improvising experience. A conductor would be superfluous in Riley's music, because all those elements that are usually controlled by a conductor, are absent from Riley's music which instead deals with dynamic nuances, tempo changes, obligatory attacks and so on; and where tempo and rhythm are concerned, performers can always fall back on the pulse.

In 1967, Riley realized *Poppy Nogood*, a work for soprano saxo-phone and time-lag accumulator, at festivals in Pennsylvania and Amagansett (Long Island, New York). (A time-lag accumulator is used to produce an artificially repeated echo, whose length can be varied). And around that time, Riley also performed *Poppy Nogood's Phantom Band Purple Modal Strobe Ecstasy* at different locations in New York, along with a group of dancers and acrobats called The Daughters of Destruction.

Terry Riley situates his music between the Western tradition and jazz. According to Riley, in the West, people tend to add too much material. On the other hand, Riley examines only a small amount of material intensively, and only when the material is exhausted does he add something new to it.

Thoug Riley has studied with the Indian master Pandit Pran Nath since 1970, one cannot find any real influence, since he came to Indian music more by thinking through his own musical ideas. This is partly proved by the fact that he does not rely on a fixed form-scheme, which is an important aspect in Indian improvisatory music.

Riley is the only one of the four composers under scrutiny whose music deviates from the principle of objectivisation of the music. While Young expressed his concern about the role of the traditional composer handling sounds to express his thoughts, Riley considers the idea of free improvisation to be an important aspect of spontaneous expression. He says that "the music has to be the expression of spiritual categories like philosophy, knowledge and truth, the highest human qualities. To realize this, my music necessarily radiates balance and rest."

15 Steve Reich

Steve Reich

Steve Reich was born in New York on 3rd October, 1936, studied philosophy at Cornell University and composition at the Julliard School of Music and at the Mills College (California), with Luciano Berio and Darius Milhaud. He remained in San Francisco for some time, where he devoted himself entirely to composition until, in 1966, when back in New York, he set up his own ensemble which has since grown from three to over twenty musicians. In fact the development of this ensemble goes hand in hand with the gradual evolution of Reich's works.

The influence of ethnic music on his compositions is strong. In 1970 he studied drumming techniques with a master drummer of the Ewe tribe in Ghana, and in 1973 and '74 he took part in a seminar on Balinese gamelan music at the University of California, Berkeley. It is no coincidence that many of the musicians in Reich's original ensemble had studied at Westleyan University, whose extensive course in ethno-musicology or world music was the first of its kind in the United States.

In 1972 and '73, Reich collaborated with the dancer/choreographer Laura Dean, with whom he gave joint performances in Europe and America. He was invited to Berlin to be an artist — as part of the DAAD scheme — and in 1974 he published his *Writings about Music*. Reich has had several important commissions, such as the one from the Holland Festival for which he composed *Music for a Large Ensemble* in 1979.

In the early part of 1980 the scores of seven works, written between 1967 and 1973, were published by Universal Edition (London).

   Steve Reich's early works are remarkable for the emphasis they put on the written word and in particular the poetry of William Carlos Williams, Charles Olsen and Robert Creeley. But he soon began to feel a lack of freedom when setting texts to music so he began using extracts from speeches, interviews, sports commentaries, etc. as the basis of a number of tape pieces, and this gave him a far greater degree of freedom in handling the spoken word. Reich had already worked with tape in the soundtrack tape he composed in 1964 for the *Plastic Haircut*, an experimental film by Robert Nelson. Following Riley's example, Reich experimented with tape loops and in 1965 he accidentally discovered the process of gradual phase shifting. His intention had been to let the same loop play against itself, but during the experiment he noted that the two tape recorders did not run at precisely the same speed and this produced a time shift between the two loops. Reich decided to elaborate this principle and continued to experiment with different loops in unison, allowing them to shift gradually out of phase with each other. This technique, along with his free use of textual snippets and his growing interest in repetition, are the most important characteristics of Reich's early works.

   It's Gonna Rain is a tape piece composed in 1965, and it uses excerpts from a speech Reich recorded of a black preacher orating about the deluge. In the first part of this work a gradual phase shifting process was applied; the second part has a more complex construction and includes more fragments from the preacher's text: "Knocking upon the door, let's showing up, Alleluia, God, I didn't see you". This series starts with two voices and is spun out by shifting the phasing of patterns until eight voices are heard. Reich describes this *phase shifting process* as "an extension of the idea of infinite canon, or round in medieval music, in which two or more identical melodies are played; one starts after the other, as in traditional rounds, but in the *phase shifting process* the melodies are usually much shorter repeating patterns, and the imitations, instead of being fixed, are variable."

   In his *Writings about Music*, Reich says that the importance of the *phase shifting process* lies in its impersonality: once the process has been set up, it inexorably works itself out, is very precise and leaves nothing to chance. *Come Out* and *Melodica* (1966) were built with the same means as *It's Gonna Rain*. *Come Out* is based on a phrase of a 19-year old boy: "I had to, like, open the bruise up and let some of the bruise blood come out to show them". This sentence is repeated three times and subjected to fragmentation through phase shifting, and in this way the piece develops from unison to an incomprehensible overlapping of text and phonetic fragments.

Melodica did not use vocal materials but uses pitches played on a melodica; this material is then worked on through a series of *tape-loops*. It has the same rhythmic structure as *Come Out* and was Reich's last tape piece before he switched to writing instrumental music.

From 1967 on, Reich applied the gradual phase shifting process to instrumental music and in that year he composed *Piano Phase* for two pianos, the first of Reich's pieces in which one can see very clearly the dualism of stasis and movement that is characteristic of repetitive music consisting of a fixed part that repeats the basic pattern throughout the piece while the second part accelerates to take it out of phase to produce an ever-changing alignment against the first part, resulting in the stressing of constantly different notes or groups of notes. The piece is built up cyclically: the second player starts playing a quaver further on in relation to the first player after each acceleration so that, eventually, after a certain number of repetitions, both players reach unison again. Three cycles are run through in this way, and each time a new cycle begins the basic motive is altered. The first melodic pattern, from which the others are derived, consists of twelve notes and uses five different pitches.

16 Figures 1-6 from *Piano Phase* (1967): phase shifting of the first melodic pattern

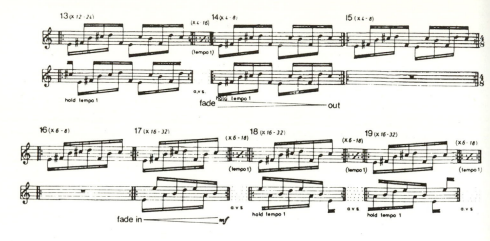

17 Figures 13-19 from *Piano Phase*: transition between the first and second sections

Piano Phase is still a fairly rudimentary work and lacks any harmonic complications. In *Violin Phase*, written in the same year, the basic melodic motive becomes more complex harmonically as well as rhythmically. It is composed for four violins but can also be performed with three pre-recorded violins and one live violin and is provided with an extensive accompanying text with performing instructions.

Violin Phase has five sections from which cyclic structure has entirely disappeared; phase shift is still used but the figures no longer return to unison. And in addition Reich introduces a second motive in this work, clearly different from the first in pitch and rhythm. What is new about the second part of *Violin Phase* is the appearance of *resulting patterns*. When one listens to the repeated figures one may hear the lower tones forming a particular pattern; then maybe the higher notes are heard to form another pattern, and after this, the medium tones may become linked to lower ones to form yet another pattern. All these patterns are created by the interlocking of two, three or four violin parts all playing the same pattern, but out of phase with each other. Because it is inevitable that the listener will hear and because, at the same time, the listener decides what he wants to hear and when, one can understand the psycho-acoustic effect of this music. Reich says: "Some of these resulting patterns are more noticeable than others, or become noticeable once they are pointed out. This 'pointing out' process is accomplished musically by doubling one of these pre-existent patterns with the same instrument, i.e. a violin in *Violin Phase*. The pattern is played very softly, and then gradually the volume is increased so that it slowly rises to the surface of the music and then, by lowering the volume, gradually sinks back into the overall texture, while remaining audible in the whole, as an integrating element in the entire sound field. The listener thus becomes aware of one pattern in the music which may open his ear to another, and another, all sounding simultaneously in the ongoing overall texture of sounds.''

The third section of *Violin Phase* starts when the resulting patterns disappear and the violins, now playing in three voices, build up a new phase shift. When violin two disappears and the third recorded or live violin starts playing, a new series of resulting-pattern begins. In the fourth section both resulting patterns and the phase shifting process are employed. The second violin plays rhythmic motives in a shifting phase relationship with the other parts which keep repeating. In the fifth and last section the phase shifting disappears and only resulting patterns are left. Changes in dynamics occur in this piece, but are hardly audible because each crescendo in one part is compensated for by a crescendo in another part, or otherwise happens very gradually.

18 Extract from *Violin Phase* (1967): resulting patterns on stave four and alternative resulting patterns on stave six

Subsequently, Reich elaborated these principles in *Phase Patterns* (1970) and in *Drumming* (1971). Chronologically speaking *Violin Phase* inaugurates a period during which Reich wrote live electronic music. He built up a system in which the phase shifting process happens so slowly that very small rhythmic differences are audible and the one pattern gradually flows into the other. In this system one first hears separate notes, played in phase, and then one part moves to its own tempo that differs only slightly from the original tempo. As an aid to the performance of this music Larry Owen built a phase varying metronome for Reich and in 1968, the *Phase Shifting Pulse Gate* was ready and was used in two electronic works of 1969, *Pulse Music* and *Four Log Drums.*

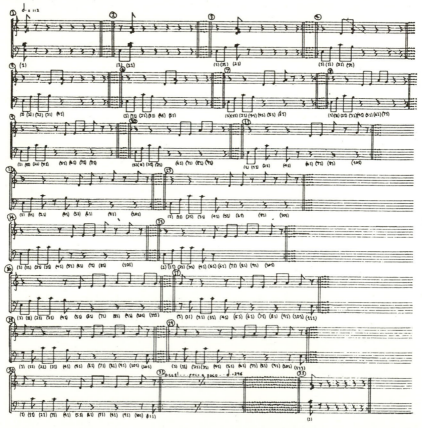

19 *Pulse Music* (1969): for Phase Shifting Pulse Gate

Reich performed *Pulse Music* for the first time at a concert in the New School in New York in 1969 and a second time in a modified form in the Whitney Museum of American Art. Eight oscillators realize eight different pitches, of which four are put through different channels, so that the *gate* has a total capacity of twelve notes. Bars 13 to 16 of this work illustrate how these undoubled notes appear in four different phase positions. The dotted lines mark the places where phase shift appears.

For the concert in the Whitney Museum, *Pulse Music* was preceded by *Four Log Drums* — its sole performance. The *gate* functioned as an instrument for programming the four performers, each playing a wooden percussion instrument with two pitches. The performers hear the pulsations the *gate* produces over headphones and their task is limited to reproducing the pulse they hear through the *gate* on their instruments. Tempo and pitch are the same as in *Pulse Music,* so the latter therefore starts immediately after bar 14 of *Four Log Drums.*

20 *Four Log Drums* (1969)

But Reich was not satisfied with the results of these electronic machines, so these compositions were soon discarded. One live electronic piece, however, *Pendulum Music* of 1968, remains from this period; it is still often performed and was published in score in 1980. In this piece three or more microphones, fed through amplifier and loudspeaker, are suspended from the ceiling at the same height, so that they can swing freely. The microphones are suspended in rest exactly above the loudspeakers so that feedback will be produced when the mike swings above the speaker. At the beginning of the performance the performers take hold of the microphones and draw them towards them. Simultaneously the performers release the microphones and as they swing over the speakers a series of feedback pulses is produced. The performers join the audience and when the microphones are still and a continuous feedback is heard they take hold of their microphones again and the piece is over. *Pendulum Music* is a clear illustration of Reich's well-known statement: "Once the process has been set up it inexorably works itself out." This also makes clear how the composer strives for impersonality and the removal of subjectivity from his music.

PENDULUM MUSIC

FOR MICROPHONES, AMPLIFIERS, SPEAKERS AND PERFORMERS

2, 3, 4 or more microphones are suspended from the ceiling by their cables so that they all hang the same distance from the floor and are all free to swing with a pendular motion. Each microphone's cable is plugged into an amplifier which is connected to a speaker. Each microphone hangs a few inches directly above or next to it's speaker.

The performance begins with performers taking each mike, pulling it back like a swing, and then in unison releasing all of them together. Performers then carefully turn up each amplifier just to the point where feedback occurs when a mike swings directly over or next to it's speaker. Thus, a series of feedback pulses are heard which will either be all in unison or not depending on the gradually changing phase relations of the different mike pendulums.

Performers then sit down to watch and listen to the process along with the audience.

The piece is ended sometime after all mikes have come to rest and are feeding back a continuous tone by performers pulling out the power cords of the amplifiers.

Steve Reich 8/68

Having discarded the phase shifting gate, Reich still retained some of the techniques he discovered through it and applied them in *Four Organs* (1970) to live musical instruments — four organs and two pairs of maracas. The maracas maintain a fast quaver pulse throughout the piece while the four organs stress certain quavers with a recurrent 11th chord. The main characteristics of this work are repetition, rhythmic changes in the organ parts based on the augmentation process and tonal writing. *Four Organs* evolves in a linear process rather reminiscent of a slow crescendo; the consonant chord continually expanded until it appears as a horizontal consonant after twenty minutes. By means of this lengthening process Reich intends to obtain *slow motion music*. The concept of this work grew out of another composition, *Slow Motion Sound* of 1967, and this carries the instruction: "Gradually slow down a recorded sound until it is many times its original length without changing pitch or timbre." For technical reasons this augmentation process was never carried out in a tape piece, but it is applied in a modified form in *Four Organs* and in *Music for Mallet Instruments, Voices and Organ* (1973). The linear evolution of *Four Organs* makes it unique in Reich's works since his other earlier works are mostly conceived cyclically: starting in unison, shifting phase and eventually returning to unison.

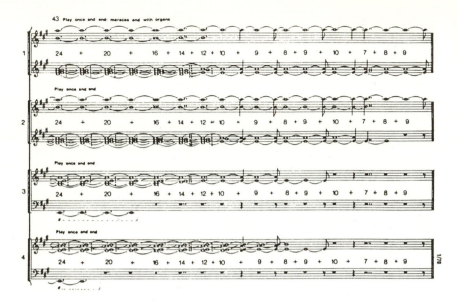

21 *Four Organs* (1970): first and last bars. The chord becomes less dense after 24 beats and entirely disappears after 156 beats

In *Phase Patterns*, also for four organs and written in the same year as *Four Organs*, Reich developed the system of resulting patterns. The keyboards are played as tuned percussion instruments in *Four Organs* but more so in *Phase Patterns*, where the technical difficulty of the keyboard writing is voluntarily highly restricted. The complexity in the work lies elsewhere, namely in the precise rhythmic relations between the different performers. This stress on the purely rhythmic element becomes more and more obvious, and this Reich affirmed when he indicated that this piece made him concentrate seriously on the study of African percussion techniques.

In *Drumming* (1970-71), Reich stresses the rhythmic construction partially by the use of percussion instruments. He wrote this piece after a study trip to Africa in June/July 1970 and the influence of African music is obvious. *Drumming* is a key work in Reich's output because it is the last one he wrote in which he uses phasing and

The first keyboard player begins and is joined in unison by the second at number 0. After about a minute of getting comfortable the second player gradually increases his tempo very slightly so that he begins to move ahead until, say in about 15–30 seconds, he is one eighth note ahead of the first performer, as shown at 1. The dotted lines indicate this gradual movement and the consequent shift of phase relation between the two performers. This one eighth note out. of phase relation is then held while the third and fourth performers bring out several patterns resulting from this combination of keyboards one and two. Six patterns of this sort are written out at 1.

22 *Phase Patterns*, bars 0–1. The process of gradually shifting phase relations between two or more identical repeating figures played on two or more identical instruments.

because he introduces a whole series of new techniques. Thus Reich uses female voices as a part of the instrumental ensemble, by making them imitate precisely the sound of the instruments. He also combines instruments with different timbres — here unmixed through his use of identical instrument groups. In *Drumming* Reich makes the timbre changes autonomously, independently of rhythm and pitch. At the opening of the first part of *Drumming* Reich introduces the technique of rhythmic construction in which rests are systematically replaced by units of sound and units of sound by rests. Thus, *Drumming* can be considered as a blueprint of almost all characteristics of Reich's later works: phase-shifting, resulting patterns, rhythmic construction and the application of the augmentation process.

23 Bars 1-8 and 93-100 from *Drumming* (1971): two performers substitute beats for rests, gradually building up the basic rhythmic pattern

Reich used sudden phase changes, as opposed to the gradual phase shifting, in some of the tape works he wrote before 1970 but he only applies it systematically after *Clapping Music*, composed in 1971 out of a desire "to write a piece of music that would need no instruments at all beyond the human body" (in this case two performers clapping their hands).

24 *Clapping Music* (1971): the basic rhythm and the first two rhythmic shifts

In this work, two identical rhythmic patterns of twelve quavers are played simultaneously in different phase positions. The phase shifts are not made gradually after twelve repetitions of the same phase relationship with each quaver, so that the original unison is reached in the thirteenth figure.

After *Clapping Music*, Reich decided to discard *phase shifting process* as a compositional technique and concentrated instead on the techniques of rhythmic construction and augmentation. From this decision, three new compositions resulted in 1973: *Six Pianos, Music for Mallet Instruments, Voices and Organ* and *Music for Pieces of Wood*. *Six Pianos* clearly illustrates the process of rhythmic construction and systematically replaces rests by sound units. Three piano players play the same eight-beat pattern, but with different notes; the two others play in a gradually evolving process and in unison one of the figures of the other players. First they play the fifth beat of the other performer on their seventh beat, then the first beat on their third beat, etc... till pianists four and five integrally perform the same pattern, but two beats out of phase. At the end of this process all the rests have been replaced by notes.

25 *Six Pianos* (1973): the first eight bars demonstrate the rhythmic construction

   Reich has said of this process that he applied it previously in
Drumming, but its use in *Six Pianos* happens, unlike *Drumming*,
between different performers playing the pattern against each other.
"The result", Reich writes, "can be compared to the *Drumming*-
technique, but the way it is obtained, is basically different." *Music for
Mallet Instruments, Voices and Organ* was finished in May 1973 and
consists of two simultaneous, interrelated rhythmic processes. The
first is the bar-by-bar building up of a duplicate of a repeating pattern
with the duplicate being one or two beats out of phase with the
original, just like in *Six Pianos*. This triggers the second process, the
augmentation of a simultaneous but different repeating pattern. The
first process is performed by marimbas against marimbas, and by
glockenspiel against glockenspiel, and to these rhythmic structures
two women's voices and organ are added. When marimba and

glockenspiel have reached their point of highest activity, and the voices and organ have stretched their values to a maximum length, a third woman's voice is added and doubles some of the melodic motives which result from the marimba parts. Then a vibraphone plays a quick, flowing semiquaver figure with marimbas and glockenspiels suddenly playing in unison, while voices and organ again reduce the length of their notes. This coupled process of rhythmic construction, augmentation and reduction to rhythmic unison occurs four times in other parts that are marked by changes in key and measure. The first part is in F dorian and 3/4, the second in A flat dorian and 2/4, the third in B flat minor and 3/4 and the fourth consists of a dominant 11th chord on A flat in 3/4.

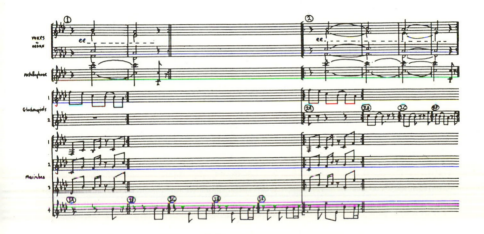

26 *Music for Mallets* (1973)

Reich's approach to the human voice in *Music for Mallet Instruments, Voices and Organ* was entirely new, and he succeeded in using the voice in such a way that its timbral quality can be called vocal as well as instrumental. In his *Writings about Music*, Reich indicated that "the imitation of instruments by human voices" was one of his main concerns in the piece; he also announced that there were a lot more possibilities in this area that he wanted to realize in later compositions.

But before concentrating on those pieces, we should look briefly at *Music for Pieces of Wood* also composed in 1973. Like *Clapping Music* this piece arose from the desire to make music with the simplest possible instruments, in this case five claves with specified pitches (A, B, C sharp, D sharp and D sharp an octave higher) played by five players with strong, resonant, attacks. In fact Reich has said of his work that "It is one of the loudest I ever composed and no form of amplification is needed. The piece can eventually be played on tuned cowbells."

The structure of this piece is once again based on the rhythmic structure where rests are systematically replaced by notes. The work is divided into three sections whose bar lengths are reduced each time: 6/4, 4/4 and 3/4.

After 1973, Reich concentrated on composing for large ensembles, resulting in two important works, *Music for 18 Musicians* (1976) and *Music for a Large Ensemble* (1979). The enlarging of Reich's performing group is accompanied by a growth in importance of psycho-acoustic by-products; in fact one even gets the impression that these effects play as important a part as the development of the process itself. But the augmentation of the harmonic and melodic material and the very precise weighting and combining of different timbre-groups is particularly noteworthy. Although *Music for 18 Musicians* harks back to Reich's earlier works, its structure, instrumentation and harmony are new. The basic material consists of a sequence of eleven chords which are heard at the beginning and the end of the work. These chords, repeated in pulsing and sustained notes for the length of two breaths of the bass clarinettists, are examined one by one over a period of five minutes as the basic harmony over which longer musical periods are later elaborated. The different sections of the work have an arch structure: A B C D C B A. The main focus in *Music for 18 Musicians* is on harmony — in fact Reich has noted that the opening of this work contains more harmonic movement than any other of his pieces. Rhythmically the work has two distinctive features: the regular pulse of piano and percussion and the rhythm of the human breathing in the vocal and wind parts, and the interaction between them brings about, according to Reich, a remarkable effect of wave motion. At the basis of the development of *Music for 18 Musicians* is the rhythmic relationship between harmony and melody. A single melody may be repeated a number of times but it can be stressed differently by the rhythm, so that ever-changing tonal harmonies appear. These rhythmic and resulting harmonic changes move against a constantly sustained melodic pattern. The vibraphone functions as a 'conductor' by indicating when the players have to switch from one section to the next, or when the harmony or melody should change within a section.

Music for a Large Ensemble had its first performance in Utrecht on June 14, 1979. The work was commissioned by the Holland Festival and performed with some of his own musicians and members of the Netherlands Wind Ensemble. Reich has said that *Music for a Large Ensemble* develops out of two previous compositions, *Music for Mallet Instruments, Voices and Organ* and *Music for 18 Musicians*. It employs more musicians than Reich had ever worked with before and includes instruments from all sections of the orchestra: strings, woodwinds, brass and percussion, to which women's voices are added. The piece is in five sections, each having a sort of A-B-C-B-A shape. At the beginning there are some shorter phrases, which grow longer by means of augmentation, and later on return to their original length by means of diminution. At which point, the key and/or time changes and the next section starts. In the middle of each section there are some longer and decorative melodic lines that can be heard in the clarinets and the first violin: these are signs of Reich's growing interest in longer and more traditionally-orientated melodies. "This interest has its roots in my earlier pieces and in my study of the singing and reciting of Hebrew writings in 1976-77," Reich has noted. And his current interest in human breathing as a measure of musical periodization accounts for the use of four trumpets in this piece. The piece can be played without conductor: "When much rehearsal time is available, one can learn to deduce, while listening, from the vibraphonist's signs when one has to move to the next bar. Thus *Music for a Large Ensemble* can be considered as a piece of chamber music for a very large ensemble", says Reich.

Octet (also composed in 1979) is evidence of Reich's continuing interest in more expansive melodic material, and this work, the subsequent *Variations for Winds, Strings and Keyboards*, along with *Music for a Large Ensemble*, formed the programme for the major Carnegie Hall concert Steve Reich gave in New York on February 19, 1980.

The Carnegie Hall Corporation presents

Steve Reich
Three New Works

Music for a Large Ensemble (1978)
Octet (1979)
Variations for Winds, Strings and Keyboards (1979)

performed by

Steve Reich and Musicians

and guest artists

Percussion	*Keyboards*	*Strings*	*Woodwinds*	*Brass*
Russ Hartenberger	Nurit Tilles	Shem Guibbory	Virgil Blackwell	David Taylor
James Preiss	Edmund Niemann	Chris Finckel	Mort Silver	Lawrence Benz
Bob Becker	Larry Karush	Michael Finckel	Richard Cohen	Douglas Hedwig
Glen Velez	Joseph Kubera	Robert Chausow	Paul McCandless	Marshall Farr
Gary Schall	Steve Reich	Ruth Siegler	Ed Joffe	James Hamlin
David Van Tieghem		Louis Paer	Vivian Burdick	James Dooley
Richard Schwarz	*Voices*	Claire Bergman	Ellen Bardekoff	Clifford Haynes
	Jay Clayton	Judith Sugarman	Vincent Gnojeck	Richard Schneider
	Elizabeth Arnold	Christine Gummere		
		Ron Lawrence		

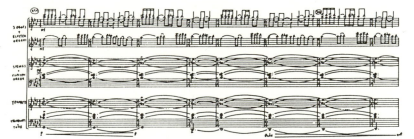

Variations for Winds, Strings and Keyboards (1979) bars 494-501

Tuesday, February 19, 1980, at 8pm
Carnegie Hall

154 West 57th Street, New York, N.Y. 10019
tickets $10.50, $9.50, $8.50, $7.00, $5.50
at Box Office or call Carnegie Charge (212) 247-7459

with support from The New York State Council on the Arts and The National Endowment for the Arts

27 Philip Glass

Philip Glass

Philip Glass was born in Baltimore, Maryland, on January 31, 1937. Initially he studied flute, then piano, harmony and composition with Louis Cheslock. After studies at the Julliard Music School he studied with Darius Milhaud (in 1960) and Nadia Boulanger (between 1964-1966) in France. During his stay in Paris, he worked on a sound track for a movie and met Ravi Shankar and his tabla player, Alla Rakka. In 1966-1967, Philip Glass stayed in Tibet and India, and during these trips his interest in non-European music grew and he paid especial attention to musical traditions based on additive structure principles. By the end of 1967, Glass had returned to the United States and settled in New York, where a year later he set up his own performing group, the Philip Glass Ensemble. His first opera, *Einstein on the Beach,* a collaboration with Robert Wilson, was given its première in Avignon in 1976. In 1971, Glass set up his own record label Chatham Square. He wrote the soundtrack for the film *North Star, Marc di Suvero,* for which he obtained a prize at the Chicago Film Festival. In response to a commission from the Holland Festival in 1977, Glass wrote an organ composition for the tenth birthday of the De Doelen organ in Rotterdam and wrote a second opera, *Satyagraha,* first performed in Rotterdam in September 1980.

Not much is known about the works Glass wrote before 1966 — some eighty compositions, of which around twenty were published, written mainly in what Glass has called "a more traditional style" and which Glass has disowned since 1968.

Glass's more personal music is based on repetition in which the musical figures are structured according to an additive method, and this method of structuring is, without any doubt, the most characteristic feature of his style. Its origin lies in Indian music, and it can be set in opposition to the Western principle of divisive time division, with longer units being subdivided into smaller units. The Indian musician, on the other hand, works with much larger units that are created by bringing smaller units together which have a structure different from that of the larger units they finally form. "These larger units or periods are integrated in a cyclical process. Other cycles with different rhythms are added afterwards like in a wheel-work: everything works simultaneously in a continuous transformation", Glass says.

Before he began to employ additive structures, Glass wrote music based on repetition and rhythmic cycles, also Indian in origin.

In *Strung Out* (1967) for electric violin and *600 Lines*, written for Glass's ensemble, this rhythmic system is developed, but the Indian

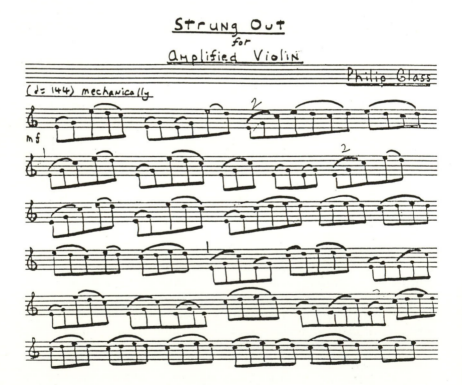

28 Opening of *Strung Out* (1967) for amplified violin

principle of additive structuring is not pursued fully. About this piece, Glass has said of *Strung Out* that it is written in a "personal style" and that it carries many of the characteristics of his later works. Its title refers to the way in which the folding score of some twenty pages is bound; it was first performed in 1968. In the structural sense, Glass calls this piece *self-revealing*. The last three notes of the melodic cell are the basis for a series of note groups that are systematically extended by the gradual addition of extra notes. This results in a number of rising and falling phrases, that are sometimes interrupted by smaller, discontinuous figures. The repetitive structure, the stable harmony and the use of continuous quavers, along with the aural rec-ognisability, reveal the basic characteristics of this later music.

The additive principle is applied further in *One + One* written in 1968. The composer uses two rhythmic cells — to be tapped in a

29 *One + One* (1968)

quick tempo by the performer on any table surface amplified by contact microphones, amplifier and loudspeaker. The rhythmic cells are repeated within one series and the series are repeated as wholes several times in a continuous, regular arithmetic progression.

In *Two Pages* of 1969, Glass used the additive structure method for the first time in an ensemble context. The music of *Two Pages, Music in Fifths, Music in Contrary Motion* and *Music in Similar Motion* comprises a number of long and short melodic figures that are augmented or reduced by the addition or omission of small melodic cells.

Two Pages is in rhythmic as well as melodic unison. Changes in timbre do not occur in the piece — once the timbre of a certain performance has been fixed, it remains constant during the whole performance. The piece is loud and dynamic. (Glass recorded the work in 1975 with electronic organ and piano).

30 Beginning and end of *Two Pages* (1969)

The melodic material of this composition is reduced to a minimum and consists of only five pitches (G, C, D, E♭ and F) and one rhythmic value (the quaver). Noteworthy are the sudden start and the unprepared end, which gives the listener the feeling that he or she only hears a fragment in a permanent musical continuum. Glass says: "The best music is experienced as one event, without start or end".

Music in Fifths, also written in 1969, differs from *Two Pages* in its addition of a second melodic line one fifth higher than the first line. Glass's purpose is to "create structures with the aid of sounds". He does not use additive processes as a formal scheme, but in order to create psycho-acoustic effects. "I believe", he says, "that the listeners in this matter are one step beyond me. Whereas I, as composer, am concerned with the structure and formal unity, the attention of my audience is mainly drawn to the sound itself. I should concentrate more on the sounding results than on formal aspects."

31 Extract from *Music in Fifths* (1969)

In 1970, Glass observed a curious acoustic phenomenon while rehearsing *Music in Similar Motion*, in a circular concert hall with wooden walls in Minneapolis. Glass noted that some sustained tones not actually sung or played arose as psycho-acoustic results of the dense instrumental texture.

Whereas the basis of Glass's earlier works was additive structure, an evolution can be seen after 1970, when he leans towards a growing vertical differentiation — the use of harmony as a structural principle. The musical texture has become richer and more differentiated through the expansion of Glass's ensemble and the concern with rhythmic structure is no longer dominant: *Two Pages* (1968) still develops in one line, *Music in Fifths* (1969) uses a parallel interval and in *Music in Contrary Motion* (1969) three parts sound together: two converging and diverging lines, and a third basic line serving as a support; *Music in Similar Motion* (1969) starts in two voices and develops, in the end (from bar 23 on), into four voices. The simple initial figures are developed differently in both pieces: in *Music in Contrary Motion*, the motives are mainly elaborated horizontally, while in *Music in Similar Motion* a step is made in the direction of harmony as a structural principle, and the vertical structure becomes richer. At the same time, this is Glass's first work in which the texture is sufficiently rich to create psyco-acoustic effects. As a result of this experience, Glass subsequently wrote *Music with Changing Parts*.

32 Beginning and end of *Music in Similar Motion* and *Music in Contrary Motion* (1969)

In *Music with Changing Parts* (1973), Glass shows some interest in the acoustic sound phenomena that result from the repetition of notes and cells, and in the sounds that result from a combination of notes played by different instruments. Furthermore, he uses *Changing figures*, indicated in the score by means of "C, F" and numbered from 1 to 11, — these indicate a (limited) form of improvisation. "In fact", says Glass, "this is an *open score* in which the parts are not fully written out: the performers play the sounds that are most proper to the musical structure of the moment". These *changing figures* force the performers, moreover, to listen to each other.

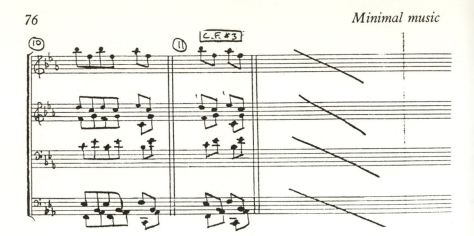

© Philip Glass 1973

33 Examples of Changing Figures (CF) and final bars from *Music with Changing Parts* (1973)

The use of modulation is a remarkable departure for Glass. After some 40 minutes, a sudden transition is made in figure 73, without any preparation or solution in a passage where the A sharps become natural. This modulation causes a feeling of transition from minor to major, but as the sense of a clear key is lacking, this could just as well be written in the dorian mode on C (C, D, E♭, F, G, A, B♭, C). This sudden modulation causes a psychological dis-orientation of the listener and contributes also to the feeling of infinity Glass's music radiates*.

Glass's interest in harmonic differentiation continues in *Music in Twelve Parts*, written between May 1971 and April 1974. In addition to the application of previously used techniques like additive process, repetitive construction, continuous quaver movement, pulsation, a stable harmony per part and the introduction of sudden modulations with each transition to a new part, Glass introduces a number of new techniques. For instance, Part 1 is notable for the presence of a perfect fifth (F♯ -C♯) that is audible continuously as a "new resulting musical pattern" but is not written as such since it is the result of a number of overlapping figures.

* It is possible that Glass influenced Reich, who did not introduce sudden modulations until *Six Pianos* of 1973.

34 Extract from *Music in 12 Parts* - Part 1 (1971)

In addition, *Music in Twelve Parts* is remarkable for its use of decorations (Part 9), the variable use of the monodic and polyphonic writing styles that provides an effect of continuously changing melodic material (Part 7), the exchange of melodic patterns between different parts, thus creating a strongly pulsing rhythm (Part 3 and the beginning of Part 4) and the use of harmonic figures functioning as a structural element, quickly following each other and having a proper development (Part 12).

With *Music in Twelve Parts* — a work that lasts four and a half hours — Glass wishes to confront the audience with a new way of listening: "The music is placed outside the usual time-scale substituting a non-narrative and extended time-sense, in its place... When it becomes apparent that nothing 'happens' in the usual sense, but that, instead, the gradual acretion of musical material can and does serve as the basis of the listener's attention, then he can perhaps discover another mode of listening — one in which neither memory nor anticipation (the usual psychological devices of programmatic music whether Baroque, Classical, Romantic or Modernistic) have a place in sustaining the texture, quality or reality of the musical experience. It is hoped that one would be able to perceive the music as a dramatic structure, pure medium 'of sound'."

The idea of harmonisation as structural element is developed by Glass in *Another Look at Harmony*, a work in four parts, composed in 1977. *Another Look at Harmony* is built on the assumption of chordal equality. Chords are used in a way that takes them outside the tonal functionalism of the classical system — that is, relatively simple chords are placed side by side in parallel on different degrees of the scale, causing the tonal relationship to disappear too. In this piece, Glass also manages to integrate harmony and rhythmic structure. Part One, for instance, consists of a series of harmonic plateaus each generating their own structure, and every key has its corresponding rhythmic structure. Another example of the link between harmony and rhythm can be found in Part Two. Here Glass starts out from an overtly traditional harmonic progression, the cadenza; after a number of repetitions, this harmonic figure is extended in a rhythmic-arithmetic manner and an additive process develops.

This overt use of harmony is the link between *Another Look at Harmony* and Glass's first opera, *Einstein on the Beach*, the 1975 collaboration with Robert Wilson.

35 Extract from *Another Look at Harmony* - Part 4, for choir and organ, commissioned by the Holland Festival, 1977

Wilson has created interest in theatrical circles in the United States for some years, not least for the unusual length of these pieces. Wilson considers his pieces as "dream-plays" in which, because of the long duration, it is impossible for the spectator to sustain a consistent attention. His pieces bring about an intermingling of external and internal experiences. It is therefore not surpriseing that Wilson should at some time have become interested in Albert Einstein, especially as Einstein discovered that time and space are not only relative for the movement of objects, but also for the observer who carries his own time and space with him.

In *Einstein on the Beach* there are two protagonists: the violin player performing Einstein, and the spectator. Dancers and actors appear as schizophrenic un-doublings of the Einstein character and are all dressed the same way.

The opera is in four acts and lasts more than five hours. There are recurrent elements: a train, a process and a space ship. The work presents a quite remarkable co-ordination between staging and music. Glass's music is characterized by a seeming immobility and an apparently infinite duration, just like Wilson's theatre. There is hardly any narrative structure — the different scenes are entirely independent, and seem to be arbitrarily shifted. The singers sing either note names (solfeggio) or numbers corresponding to the length of the note. Simple rhythmic patterns, short melodic motives that are infinitely repeated and simple harmonic progressions are the most typical features of the music. The most important theme is characterized by the rhythmic development of a cadential formula, and in fact this cadenza provides the basic material of the whole opera — it is used in the second, third and fourth Knee Play and provides the main body of the music in the third scene of the fourth act.

Thus *Einstein on the Beach* is an important link in the musical project that Glass began in the spring of 1975 while writing *Another Look at Harmony*: harmonic structure has to be directly linked to the rhythmic structure which itself has to be strongly featured. In traditional Western music, melody and harmony have always had priority over rhythm. In Glass's music, the prior consideration however is the rhythmic structure, to which harmony and melody must comply. Parts One and Two of *Another Look at Harmony* are the foundation of the first and second scene of the first act of the opera and they are the starting point from which the material for the other parts is developed.

36 Violin Music from *Einstein on the Beach* (1976)

37 Themes from *Einstein on the Beach*

After this opera Glass wrote another work entitled *Modern Love Waltz*. This waltz for piano solo, of 1977, is dedicated to Constance De Jong and published in *Waltzes by 25 Contemporary Composers* (Peters, 1978).

In the same year Glass wrote various compositions for the film *Northstar: Mark Di Suvero**; a choir work for the Holland Festival in 1977; an organ work for the tenth anniversary of the Doelen organ in Rotterdam (1978); and *Satyagraha*, an opera in three acts which had its première in 1980 in the Netherlands Opera in Rotterdam. Glass wrote this opera in collaboration with Constance De Jong.

for Constance De Jong
Modern Love Waltz

PHILIP GLASS
(1977)

38 Extract from *Modern Love Waltz* (1977)

---

* Fragments from *Northstar* were released in 1979 in a disco version by Mike Oldfield on the LP *Platinum* (Virgin).

39 Extract from *Satyagraha* (1980): Act 1, Scene 1, Part 1. Opening bars presenting
    the F minor, E flat, D flat and C chord progression which forms the harmonic
    base for the first act

40 Extract from *Satyagraha*: the same chord progression in enlarged orchestration at fig. 77 in the first part. The additive structure principle enlarges the progression from 5/8 (the smallest bar) to 17/8; the passage at fig. 77 represents the longest rhythmic unit in the first act.

Mahatma Gandhi is the main character in *Satyagraha*. The opera covers the period (1833-1914) during which Gandhi was in South Africa. Besides Gandhi, Tolstoi, Tagore and Martin Luther King — all known for their pacifistic ideas — appear in the play. The libretto is based on Bhagavad-Gita and is sung in the original Sanskrit. The Bhagavad Gita was an inspiration for Gandhi, it was a guide for good leadership. Satyagraha is the name which Gandhi gave to his passive resistance movement (*Satya* meaning truth and love and *Agraha* meaning strength).

During an interview with the composer in New York in June 1979, he told the author that he is working on a third opera dealing with historical figures of Egyptian history which he intends to be performed simultaneously with *Einstein on the Beach* and *Satyagraha*.

Basic concepts of minimal music

The differences one can find in the compositional techniques that Young, Riley, Glass and Reich use, in no way obscure the broad similarities in the basic mechanics of their music and its ideological connotations. These are most easily delineated by setting them against the traditional romantic-dialectical musical model.

There is only a very tenuous polemical relationship between repetitive music and romantic-dialectical music — in fact, the guiding principles of the latter have simply been ignored. But on the other hand, it is clear that repetitive music can be seen as the final stage of an anti-dialectic movement that has shaped European avant-garde music since Schoenberg, a movement that reached its culmination with John Cage, even though his music has a very obvious polemical-intellectual background and orientation completely absent from repetitive music. So, bearing in mind the way in which repetitive music had adopted certain avant-garde ideas, it is possible to evaluate critically the struggle between the avant-garde and the dialectical model. Thus the real importance of repetitive music lies in the way in which it represents the most recent stage in the continuing evolution of music since Schoenberg.

One can, of course, approach the phenomenon of repetitive music from a number of different angles — for instance, one could focus on the restorative features of its musical language, such as the restoration of tonality or the emphasis on rhythmic pulse, or the choice of easily-recognisable sound images. But such an approach seems superficial and defensive, because no matter how consistently composers of repetitive music have spoken out against the intellectualism of the avant-garde (which for Reich, includes Webern and Cage), they cannot escape its influence.

Another possible line of investigation would have been to draw attention to the open influence of non-European, so-called primitive music. La Monte Young has been influenced by Japanese Gagaku-theatre and Indian raga music and he and Terry Riley are both disciples of the Indian raga master Pandit Pran Nath. Philip Glass has based his rhythmic systems on the additive time-structures of tabla music and Steve Reich had adopted certain rhythmic principles from the music of Ghana and the Ivory Coast, and also from Balinese Gamelan music. But this use of non-European techniques should not be regarded as the foundation of their work, but rather as a symptom of the ability of the modern culture industry to annex a foreign culture, strip it of its specific social-ideological context and incorporate it into its own culture products.

In the analysis which follows, traditional dialectical music will be compared and contrasted with non-dialectical repetitive music from a number of different viewpoints. For instance, one finds that in repetitive music the concept of *work* has been replaced by the notion of *process*, and that no one sound had any greater importance than any other. And as Ernst Albrecht Stiebler wrote: "It is a characteristic of repetitive music that nothing is being expressed: it stands only for itself."

Traditional dialectical music is representational: the musical form relates to an expressive content and is a means of creating a growing tension; this is what is usually called the 'musical argument'. But repetitive music is not built around such an 'argument'; the work is non-representational and is no longer a medium for the expression of subjective feelings. Glass has written that "This music is not charac-terized by argument and development. It has disposed of traditional concepts that were closely linked to real time, to clock-time. Music is not a literal interpretation of life and the experience of time is different. It does not deal with events in a clear directional structure. In fact there is no structure at all". And additionally, that "Music no longer has a mediative function, referring to something outside itself, but it rather embodies itself without any mediation. The listener will therefore need a different approach to listening, without the tra-ditional concepts of recollection and anticipation. Music must be listened to as a pure sound-event, an act without any dramatic structure."

In the *Village Voice*, Ron Rosenbaum, the critic, wrote of an anti-apocalyptical music with an extra-historical experience of time, brought about by discarding teleological and dramatic elements. La Monte Young has removed finality, the apocalypse, from his music, and what is left is mere duration and stasis, without beginning or end: eternal music. In fact, Young has said that his *Dream House* project is a permanent, continuous work that has no beginning and goes on indefinitely.

The conventional idea of the musical work as a totality is no longer valid, since a repetitive work is essentially a process, a music whose function is not to represent something outside itself but only to refer to its own creation. Stoianova has spoken of "...generating the present at each moment. Aimless wandering without beginning, multi-directional motion without cause or effect." And, of course, this omni-directionality makes causal relationships impossible. A work becomes a process when it relates only to itself. The most important characteristic of musical process as defined by Reich is that it determines simultaneously both the note-to-note details and the overall form. Reich believes in the work's gradual inevitability: "Once the process is set up and loaded, it runs by itself." Subjective intervention is strictly ruled out in favour of a complete determinacy. Reich calls this a particularly liberating and impersonal ritual — he nominally controls everything that happens in the compositional process but also accepts everything that results without further modification. Like Reich, Glass rejects any structure that exists outside the musical process — the process has to generate its own structure: "My music has no overall structure but generates itself at each moment."

In process music, structure is secondary to sound; the two coincide only in so far as the process determines both the sound and the overall form. Repetitive music is mono-functional and sounds are not programmed to achieve a final solution of the opposition between material and structure. In dialectical music the real drama lies in the opposition between form and content and the final resolution of this opposition. But with the removal of logical causality sound becomes autonomous, so that in a process work no structure exists before sound: *it* is produced at each moment. Reich has said that he readily accepts any unplanned acoustical effects that arise in the course of the process. These are also important to Glass who said that "What is important is the immediate physiological effect on the listener." And La Monte Young, in particular, experimented with these physiological effects; he wrote about the *Well-Tuned Piano*, his most far-reaching attempt to systematize these effects, "that each harmonic interval determines a distinct feeling." What he had in mind was to make a catalogue of intervals and the feelings they produce, so as to be able to calculate a measurable effect that could be made on the listener.

In repetitive music perception is an integral and creative part of the musical process since the listener no longer perceives a finished work but actively participates in its construction. Since there is no absolute point of reference a host of interpretative perspectives are possible. So that goal-directed listening, based as it is on recollection and anticipation, is no longer suitable and must be in favour of a random, aimless listening, traditional recollection of the past being replaced by something akin to a 'recollection into the future', actualisation rather than reconstruction. This 'forward recollection' removes memory from its privileged position.

Stoianova called this a game of 'iterative monadism': what matters is not what the sound may stand for but its physiological intensity, or, as Young puts it: "One must get inside the sound".

American repetitive music is an objective music in that, since no physiological tension is created, there is an ambiguous relationship with the listener. The music exists for itself and has nothing to do with the subjectivity of the listener. The latter's position has become an ambiguous one: on the one hand he is is freed of intentionality, but on the other hand he is reduced to a passive rôle, merely submitting to the process. Reich had this in mind when he remarked that one can control everything only as long as one is prepared to accept everything.

What is more important: freedom or manipulation? Liberating the listener does not seem to be a major concern of repetitive composers. Since each moment may be the beginning or the end, the listener can choose how long he wants to listen for, but he will never miss anything by not listening. Some people have commented on the bulldozer effect of repetitive music, but this effect is erroneous since repetitive music has brought about a reversal of the traditional position; the subject no longer determines the music, as it did in the past, but the music now determines the subject. This reversal results in a shift towards extra-musical elements. For unlike traditional dialectical music, repetitive music does not represent a physical event but is the actual embodiment of this event.

Though Reich and Glass are somewhat less outspoken about the importance of the aural result, for Young and Riley, this aural result is music's only raison d'être. Riley's accumulative processes assume a fundamental distinction between micro-level and macro-level.

Continuous change is achieved by inserting new elements into the basic form that is repeated and the pulse displaces attention away from the details of form towards the overall process, so that extreme variations on the micro-level may paradoxically produce an impression of immobility. The very rapid patterns that Riley uses produce slow movements that nevertheless feel like a "vibrating motionless trance", which resembles, as Stiebler noted, a state of weightlessness, which is precisely the effect that Riley intends to achieve. In fact he has said that he considers his music has failed if it cannot bring the listener out of himself. But the opposite process is also possible: La Monte Young has used the static dimension of music as a means of producing in the listener the feeling of motion.

To what extent the adoption of a mystical ideology is an inevitable by-product of the use of repetition is not too clear, though the use of non-European musical elements has certainly led Riley and Young to come under the influence of Eastern ideology. To Riley and Young the aim of music is to get 'far out', or as Young put it: "If people don't get carried away by my music it is a failure." For Riley, pulse is a somewhat Eastern method of getting 'far out': "You can get as far out as you want by relating to a constant." And the effect of Riley's music is achieved by identification with what he calls the total time process. But the continuous variation in Riley's accumulative process negates itself because of its emptiness and leads one to perceive passing time simply as stasis. Young, on the other hand, refers to identification with sound as such: "To get into the sound: The sound is God, I am the sound that is God." The extended static sounds of La Monte Young's music suggest an anti-apocalyptic time as pure duration. Or as Wolfgang Burde wrote: "Minimal music has discovered the adventure of macro-time and what is required is no longer an analytical approach, but a surrendering to a musical stream that will lead to a new expanded experience of time." Daniel Caux made a similar point when he noted in Riley's music an attempt to hypnotize the listener back into a state of innocence.

For Glass and Reich, the removal of dialectical content from music is in no way connected with mystical ideology. Reich's music assumes neutrality of values as a matter of principle. And while his attempt to use Western sound material in the context of non-Western structural methods seems at first sight to be merely a technical procedure without ideological relevance, the fact that both his and Glass's music takes place in non-dialectical macro-time, brings them very close to the mysticism of Riley and Young. Glass has expressed his opposition to traditional clock-time and denies structured time-relationships and intentionality. In Western music, the musical argument is the result of a dialectical subdivision of time. Yet both Riley and Reich have eliminated this historical negativity: their idea of time is an empty one, and because of this no real change can take place in their music, so that a higher level of macro-time, beyond history, is reached, which has been called *now* or *stasis* or *eternity*. It is this non-historical character of repetitive music that is the real negation of subjectivity. Repetitive music attempts to unite the historical subjet with non-historical time and it is in this way that repetitive music refers to the mythical ending of history. As the sleeve note of Riley's *Rainbow in Curved Air* says: "And then all wars ended. Arms of every kind were outlawed and the masses gladly contributed them to giant foundries in which they were melted down and the metal poured into the earth. (...) All boundaries were dissolved. (...) The energy from dismantled weapons provided free heat and light. (...) The concept of work was forgotten."

This utopian view of the end of history is reflected in the absolute unity of form and content. The abolition of form-negativity implies the abolition of history itself. But in terms of actual historical reality, a far cry from the utopian world Riley envisages, this unity of form and content is pure fiction and can only be reached by denying the historical dimension of music. The use of non-Western structural principles in repetitive music is evidence of the distinction between form and the historical-ideological context that accounts for its existence. Unity of form and content is a symptom of musical positivism and identification with macro-time is nothing but historical conservatism. This absolute affirmation of reality as it is, appears to be the extra-historical realisation of subjective freedom. Yet the freedom this music claims to offer is merely freedom from history as such. It is therefore a negative freedom, paradoxically made possible only by a total addiction to history.

2 The historical development of basic concepts

As we have seen, two aspects of American repetitive music are particularly significant: the replacement of the work-as-object by the work-as-process, and the unity of form and content. The analysis which follows proposes to demonstrate how these characteristics grew out of musical developments in the earlier part of the century, which saw that progressive decline in the importance of dialectical principles. Paradoxically, the disappearance of the concept of work-as-object seems to have resulted from the absolute autonomy of the work. This autonomy, advocated by Schoenberg, Webern and post-serialist composers, resulted in the denial of the subject. In addition, the autonomous work is marked by extreme duality of form and content and its attempt to produce a strictly objective music, by means of the total control of sound material. Sound thus became atomized and, freed from a controlling structure became autonomous and this autonomy has been developed further by Cage and the composers of repetitive music. By renouncing control, aleatoricism succeeded in achieving objectivity of sound where serialism had failed because of its continued insistence on the duality of form and content.

T.W. Adorno, in his *Philosophy of New Music*, was the first writer to systematize the crisis of the concept of the work-as-object. He took the music of Schoenberg as his starting point (though much of what he wrote is more appropriate to Webern), and maintained that it suffered from a fundamental ambiguity. Because of his dependence on the romantic ideology, Schoenberg felt that the objectivisation of music is a development which represents a loss of content. Adorno calls Schoenberg's work critical, because although Schoenberg saw the growing inadequacy of the concept of work, he was at the same time unable to reject it. Webern removed the romantic elements from Schoenberg's musical thinking and in doing so removed the contra-diction within the work, having the work to isolate itself and interiorize its own conflicts.

Arnold Schoenberg

Critique of the work and work as a critique

Adorno wrote in 1949: "The only important works today are works that can no longer be regarded as works." With Schoenberg the musical work had disintegrated into fragments. Music was no longer a question of aesthetic values but of moral values. Music could no longer be convinced of its good conscience when confronted with the historical crisis. In *Doktor Faustus* Thomas Mann asked: "Can a work of art, as a purely aesthetic object, still have a meaningful relation in our complete uncertainty, our problems and the lack of harmony in our existence? Has not all art become illusion? And is not even the most marvellous illusion a lie? Illusion and playfulness confront art's conscience and desire to become knowledge." Music thus acquired a critical dimension, taking the subject/object contradiction as a starting point. The contradictions in society at large are mirrored in the contradictions of form and content, of idea and structure. Adorno wrote that "closed works assume identity of subject and object, and that this identity is an illusion, and knowledge, balancing subject and object is the greater moral value." Initially, the increased expressive potential that atonality gave the composer caused the unity of the work to decrease, and set in motion an eventual disintegration in which the specific and the general, part and whole, became irreconciliable. And this increase in expressive potential demanded an increase in structural organization. And although dodecaphony consolidated these subjective dynamics it could not bring about a real reconciliation: the form/content duality remained intact. The 12-tone technique brought about an equalisation of the musical content. As Herman Sabbe has written: "The aesthetic equalization of the musical content is the result of a growth in development technique. Each part is considered as a variation of the general organisational principle."

This equalization was already apparent in the form and pitch parameters. of atonality; dodecaphony applied this pitch equalization
consistently. In the 12-tone system form is completely determined
but this determinacy is imposed externally and remains strictly
outside the musical material, or as Adorno put it: "Music becomes
the result of a process that determines the music without revealing
itself."

In this manner the total determination of sound led paradoxically
to the internal levelling and atomizing of the material. Since structure
does not grow from a developmental process, since it is determined
from outside the material, it remains foreign to it. Totalitarian
development excludes all articulation of form and brings about its
haphazard fragmentation. The predetermined manipulation of the
tone rows excludes almost all possibility of subjective interventions
and this means that the form falls apart, making any real development
of the material impossible. Adorno states: "When all notes are
completely determined by the structure of the whole, the difference
between the essential and the inessential is obliterated. At all times
this music is equidistant from its centre. There can no longer be any
transition between essential moments, between one theme and the
next and hence themes can no longer exist, and nor, strictly speaking,
can development." The unity of part and whole was achieved in
dodecaphony at the cost of isolating the parts, because the whole does
not grow organically out of the parts but is imposed from outside;
hence, the parts break up and the whole becomes fragmented. The
principle of the general differentiation of material destroys itself,
since the predominance of variation excludes any real change. The
relationships between pitch elements and form elements are reduced
to random permutational sequences.

Schoenberg's music has been described as dissonant. Dissonance
stands for the ultimate emancipation of the romantic subject (atonality) which is, however, denied by the dodecaphonic principle of the
series. Extreme subjectivity leads to objective equalization. The
subject determines the music with a rational system but becomes
itself an object in this system. The uniformity of the material in the
series makes expression impossible and leads to subjective indifference.
All the elements of the style that the composer employs to express his
individuality are thus neutralized. Expressive content disappears, or
rather becomes fragmented and can no longer be described as subjective expression. Adorno writes: "The origin of music, like its end,

lies beyond the composer's intention, beyond meaning and beyond
subjectivity. Music becomes a gesture, a gesture close to weeping."
Schoenberg's pathos is thus the expression of the denied subject
crushed by the objective order.

Webern and post-serialism

The autonomy of the work

Adorno said that "The real abdication of the subject began with Webern." Schoenberg's contradiction, which was at the root of his pathos, has been removed: the subject is exteriorized in the object, and the object becomes subject. As Dieter Schnebel noted: "Both subject and object have been incorporated in the autonomous structure of the work." Schoenberg's pathos resulted from the process itself. The work interiorizes historical contradictions: "Webern solves dialectically the contradiction in Schoenberg's work between progressive subject and regressive object in so far as he includes regression in his own work. He reduces the progression/regression contradiction in favour of equalizing historical material. (...) Webern's work is a game of history. Schoenberg saw himself as progressive, and regression as being in the world outside himself," Schnebel has written.

In serial music the social process is neutralized. Serialism reflects a social situation where the subject is neutralized because of its impotence in the face of the objective order. For Schoenberg serialism was a method, whereas for Webern it was a generalized paradigm. For Webern the equalization that Adorno spoke about is fully realized — musical parameters are autonomous and of equal value, making any idea of hierarchy impossible. The 12-tone system tends towards the maximum determination of the material, which results in non-sensual relationships. Dissonance loses its significance because of its generalised application: through its lack of contrast with consonance, dissonance is forced to neutralise itself. Serialism extended dodecaphonic technique, originally applied only to the pitch parameter, to the parameters of timbre and intensity. After the second world war electronic music attempted to set up an integral sound control by investigating the material characteristics of sound, and consequently the material and structure are at one. Dieter Schnebel remarked that in this case form is not imposed externally but is produced by the disposition and the processes of the material. Works are no more than realisations which are determined by the chosen material and they produce their form simply through the unfolding of the material.

With this total identification of form and material, post-serialism reached its highest degree of determinacy; a process which let to the atomization of the material, and to the understandable label 'pointillism'. And, in the same way, the extreme differentiation of micro-forms resulted in a decrease in the differentiation of the material as perceived by the listener.

In a completely determined system there can be no centre, or rather the centre is everywhere and nowhere, so that the unity of the work fragmented. The post-serial work developed a kind of plural "perspectivism" that differs radically from the traditional dialectical teleology, because it excludes the possibility of dialectical synthesis. A goal-directed approach is no longer feasible because all perspectives are legitimate thus it is no longer possible to reach the ultimate goal, i.e. the *work*. Equally absent now are the work's unique point of view which does not exist any more, and its hierarchy of parameters.

Henri Pousseur took the notion of the field from physics. A field presents no causal or dialectical relationships and contains no contradictions. There are, at best, discontinuities between relative, mutually determined and polarized tendencies that cannot be reduced to one single identity. In his article *Vers un nouvel Univers Sonore*, Pousseur wrote: "Since the only relation between terms is that of mutual definition, the listener is compelled to relate to an endless network of relationships. He is to determine his own position and gather as many points of reference as possible." In other words, there is no longer a unique, exclusive way of listening; together with the multitude of perspectives, the work becomes a multitude of works — it loses its uniqueness and 'looks' different from each position, each focus and since there is an infinite number of possible positions, the work becomes *infinite*.

Stockhausen

Moment form or the infinite work

Karlheinz Stockhausen's development of *Moment-form* was a logical continuation of the notion of pluri-perspectivism of serial music and finally destroyed the concept of the work: "The work has become hyperconcentrated, as though concentric pressure has been applied to the material, until it has become so dense that it must explode and liberate its energy. The infinite form creates ever-new forms that merge with all others."

Moment-form is an open and infinite form which Stockhausen distinguishes from closed form. The latter is characterized by exposition, development and recapitulation, and by the strict dialectical principles of beginning and ending. In an open form work, the duration of performance and the duration of perception do not necessarily coincide. The duration of the performance is in fact of no importance: various durations can exist for the same piece, since beginning and ending are left open. ("The piece could have continued without ending," wrote Stockhausen.) In addition, the listener is free since he no longer needs to follow the psychic tension of the work: "The listener can come and go whenever he wishes to."

Stockhausen's *Moment-form* is based on intensities, no precise line of development can be predicted and each moment may be one of minimal or maximal intensity. Only the experience of the moment is important. This situation comes very close to Stoianova's definition of repetitive music as a monadic music. The work as it is performed is but a fragment of a more permanent work: "These pieces have always existed and will go on forever." Stockhausen rejected dialectical time, so characteristic of traditional Western music, in favour of the actual time of the moment. He stated that: "Either every moment is important or nothing is important. A moment is not simply the result of preceding moments, nor the anticipation of moments to come. It is a personal, centred entity, with its own existence. A moment is not a fraction of a time-line, not a particle lasting a measured length of time. Instead, concentration on the *now* makes vertical incisions in the horizontal line of time to reach timelessness, which is what I call eternity: an eternity that does not begin where time has ended but that can be reached at any moment." Concentration on the *now* leads, as it does in repetitive music, to an extrapolation, a macro-time beyond history, "a tendency to surmount finite time and death", says Stockhausen.

The rejection of dialectical time led Stockhausen, particularly after 1960, to an ever more outspoken mysticism. But Stockhausen did not relinquish the form/content duality. *Moment-form* differs from the repetitive sound monad in that it is still a structure conglomerate of sounds and not a sound in itself. Stockhausen called this conglomerate a 'cluster': "not a developing sequence, but an undirected use of process brings about an absolute unity of form and content, of structure and material". Thus this music requires a fundamentally different mode of listening. And as the concept of the work disappears, leading, in the case of Reich and Glass, to neutrality of values, and in the case of Young and Riley, to mystical ideology.

Since the beginning of the 17th century, Western music has been characterized by logical-causal development and by climax as the moment of teleological finality. Through contradictions that are dialectically integrated — through harmony, melody, rhythm, density and intensity, etc., — the work creates a physiological tension that grows towards a climax and then dissolves in relaxation. Repetitive music has no such obvious directionality: it does not progress along a straight, logical line but may shift suddenly from one synchrony to the next (Glass), may move through a process of gradual phase shifting (Reich), or may be completely lacking in directionality (Young).

In addition, a repetitive work has no real beginning and no real end, but instead a series of random starting and finishing points. Nor is there a gradual building up of tension or evolution towards a climax, but rather what Ivanka Stoianova has called a monadic sound intensity, where each moment and each sound is a centre in itself. Moreover, repetitive music lacks a dialectical hierarchy and thus time-field. Serialism had expanded the permutational indifference of dodecaphony but it was impossible to control rationally which permutations were likely to occur or in what sequence. Thus serialism brought about its own opposite: aleatoricism, that is, music based on chance operations. A situation has thus arisen in which only a dynamic which is externally imposed on the immobilized material is now possible; thematic development has become impossible and is replaced by indeterminacy, and dialectical development is replaced by random development.

However, in serialism indeterminacy must necessarily remain a marginal factor because it has to be submitted to the coherence of the whole. So one cannot really speak of a genuine aleatoricism in the case of John Cage, but rather what Sabbe has called a *variable form* or a *trans-serial aleatoricism*: "Trans-serial aleatoricism attempts to reconcile the concentration on the moment with the coherence of the whole into which these moments are to be transcendentally incorporated, through the rational action of the composing individual. Cage, on the other hand, attempts to avoid all disruption of this concentration and attempts to preserve the aural result from the intervention of the creating person." Serial music denies the composing subject since it obliterates itself in the autonomy of the composed work; whereas for Cage, the composing subject disappears and the work becomes objective. One can no longer speak of the *work* as such.

John Cage

The objective work

The thinking of John Cage and that of the composers of repetitive music has been influenced by serialism. These composers no longer show any interest in serial structure, but they are interested in its aural result, in so far as it is contradictory to its open structure. As has been shown, serialism leads to an unexpected autonomy of sound, which weakens the internal teleology of the work.

Christian Wolff wrote: "Complexity tends to reach a point of neutralization, continuous change results in a certain sameness. The music has a static character and goes in no particular direction. There is no necessary concern with time as a measure of distance from a point in the past to a point in the future, with linear continuity alone." It is now not only teleology that has become threatened, but the very status of the work as well. In autonomous music there is no longer a dialectic capable of producing a synthesis of the basic contradictions between form and content. Form and content thus fall apart, and the irreconcilable duality that ensues threatens the work itself.

This duality was taken as the starting point for Cage and the composers of repetitive music. The collapse of the concept of work is not regarded as a failure but rather as one more step towards the autonomy of the work. When Cage called for "an art which imitates nature in its manner of operation", he did not want a break with nature, but simply a more radical concept of the autonomy of the work.

This is also what Webern had in mind when he spoke about "a work of nature and not a creation of man". Aleatoricism maintains the serialist obsession with objectivity, but from an opposite point of view: objectivity is no longer the result of the total control of sound but can only be achieved by abandoning control and by putting the act of composing between brackets. Hence, paradoxically, the work can only be truly autonomous and objective to the extent that it ceases to be a work.

In a sense therefore, aleatoricism and serialism embody totally contradictory, yet largely parallel tendencies. Pierre Boulez had already noted this in an article he wrote in 1952, in which he characterized serialism and aleatoricism as parallel opposites. According to Boulez, each note in Cage's music has its own individuality which is not affected by the progression of the composition, so that these notes can remain neutral: "For Cage, the individual sound is an invariable entity that in the end produces a comprehensive hierarchical neutrality in the frequency range."

Serialism itself took neutrality as its starting point, but only to wind up with endless differentiation. In his study on serialism, Sabbe also noted a common perspective: "Cage deals with discontinuity and the ensuing indeterminacy through underdetermination, while serialists achieve this by overdetermination. The one provides for nearly nothing, while the other provides for so much that anything becomes possible at any moment." In serial music indeterminacy is the paradoxical result of over-organization, while for Cage it is the result of non-organization.

Aleatoricism achieves musical objectivity at the expense of the work as such. A musical work necessarily presupposes a composing subject. Serialism has rejected this subject as expressive content but not as a composing subject. Hence, serialism has less connection with objectivity than it has with the self-negation of the subject that submits to the autonomy of the composition. Genuine objectivity goes further than that and requires the negation of the composing subject itself. Leonard B. Meyer said that: "Only when art ceases to be teleological, can it become like nature: objective and impersonal." But work and subject need each other: without a composing subject the notion of the work becomes empty. Instead of a musical content, Schoenberg introduced a musical argument, and this, according to Jean-François Lyotard, was replaced by Cage, in turn, with intensity. The development of musical objectivity and autonomy can be summarized as follows: in traditional dialectical music, musical form is considered to be the representation of a subjective content, the music is a *musica ficta*. In autonomous music (dodecaphony) content is separated from the subject, through the notion of the objective musical form, but at the same time, the dialectic as form-dualism has been conserved: it is a *musica fingens*. Cage's aleatoricism goes beyond the opposition of form and content and the work no longer has a dialectical unity: aleatoricism is a *musica figura*: music that represents nothing, but refers only to itself. Dialectical negativity ceases to exist: form and content have become one.

From dialectical time to macro-time

John Cage's professed programme was "to free sound of all psychic intentionality. Sound is sound and man is man. Let sound be itself, rather than a vehicle of human theory and feeling." Cage's colleague, Christian Wolff, saw "...sound come into its own. The 'music' is a resultant existing simply in the sounds we hear, given no impulse by expressions of self or personality. It is indifferent in motive, originating in no psychology, nor in dramatic intentions, nor in literary or pictorial purposes. For at least some of these composers, then, the final intention is to be free of artistry and taste. But this need not make their work 'abstract', for nothing is denied in the end. It is simply that personal expression, drama, psychology and the like are not part of the composer's initial calculation: they are at best gratuitous." Wolff wants to do away with representation in music: "...because the intention would be circumscribed, when so many other forces are evidently in action in the final effect."

This move towards musical objectivity becomes more evident when considered in relation to time in the way it was handled by Earle Brown, and particularly by Morton Feldman — setting out to disrupt the dialectical continuity of music by removing all teleological and logical elements: "I make one sound and then I move on to the next," he has said. Traditional causality is replaced by an atomized succession. To Feldman, music is "unstructured time", the real object of composition is to deal directly with time. The emancipation of sound, that Cage and Wolff spoke about, thus shifts in emphasis to the emancipation of time itself. Earle Brown even said that "the emancipation of time is far more important than the emancipation of sound. One should compose as little as possible because the more one composes the more one gets in the way of time becoming the governing metaphor of music."

In aleatoric music, time becomes the most important structural element. However, this is not a dialectical time, but pure metrical time, so that qualitative progression has been replaced by quantitative succession, and teleological continuity has completely vanished. Using time as a structural determinant, Cage reduced the traditional dialectical opposition between form and content into the opposition of silence and sound, music thus being created by filling empty spaces of time. For Cage, form and content are separate entities: form can exist without content and content can exist without form. Structure is in no way determined by the material, but is empty and form becomes a mere assembling, a growing accumulation of isolated sounds taken out of logical context. Similarly development is impossible because sounds are merely juxtaposed and retain their identity. Nor is there a central focus since each sound is simultaneously centre and perspective. Music no longer offers a series of rationalized goal-directed relationships, but is totally determined by the point of view of the perceiver. Any sound can be the beginning, the continuation or the end, and no sound is more important than the next. The exclusive musical perspective found in dialectical teleology has been replaced by a randomly selected perspective, a phenomenon which Cage called 'interpenetration'. By this he meant that every musical element in time and space is related to every other musical element, has an equal value and works in all directions at the same time, without the existence of cause-and-effect relationships. The fact that each sound has the same value implies equally that each sound has no value. Cage sees sound only as a fragment in the time-continuum. Metrical time is thus essentially an empty time in which moments remain unfilled and neutral because they do not progress any more.

Instead of the existential identification with dialectical time that one finds in traditional music, or the neutralization of time that occurs in autonomous music, Cage identifies with macro-time, which transcends history and can therefore be called mythic. The nature of macro-time is essentially static, and duration is an atomized conglomerate of moments, without relation to past or future. As Christian Wolff said: "It is not a question of getting anywhere, of making progress, or having come from anywhere in particular, of tradition or futurism. There is neither nostalgia nor anticipation." In aleatoric music, the removal of dialectical content coincides logically with the removal of history.

Music as process

With Cage, music became experimental because the introduction of chance operations made its outcome unpredictable. Experimental composers do not deal with well-defined time-objects, but rather they outline a situation, a field in which sound may occur. What is important is not the product but the production process. In this context Schnebel uses the term *Kompositionsprozesse*: "It is not the aural effect that is prescribed, but the process that generates it."

In a traditional dialectical work, unity is ensured because product and process are the same. But dodecaphony introduced the separation of product and production process because the compositional process was no longer present in the work but preceded it. The choice of the series was made outside the composition of the work and was not determined by it; it was fortuitous.

This separation affects the unity of the work as well. Cage pushes fortuitousness to its limits by removing all subjectivity from the compositional process. So all decisive factors are withdrawn from the composing subject, and this is realized through aleatoric procedures. The notion of uniqueness is contained in the aleatoric procedure, which turns the work into a unique and unrepeatable event. Each different performance can be viewed as a new realization of a work which remains unfinished since new realizations of it can always be made. Each realization produces the work for the first time, so that it is no longer a question of *reproduction* but one of *actualization*.

The composer no longer defines relationships between sounds since these are brought about by chance through operations with the composer limiting himself to outlining a field in which such sounds may occur. The composer may indicate relationships that leave a wide margin for chance to intervene in the moment of performance. This does not mean that the performer determines the actual relationships, as is the case with improvisation, since this would be nothing more than a means of displacing the problem. Chance events cannot be controlled by the performer any more than they can by the composer.

Cage made the distinction between "that old music you speak of which has to do with dealing with *conceptions* and their *communication*, and this new music which has nothing to do with communication of concepts, only to do with *perception*." For Cage, music is physical production and perception of sounds; because perception is the basis of the work, the work becomes open and, as the environment penetrates the music, it becomes incorporated with it.

The problem of the opposition between art and reality is thus reversed and solved from within. "Art has erased the dividing line between life and art. Now it is up to life to erase the dividing line between life and art," wrote Cage. The open work adopts the utopian identification of life with art. Music has an openness to reality and seeks the end of its existence as a separate category. For Cage, music fulfils itself when it teaches people how to listen, so that they may end up preferring the trivial noises of daily life to music.

Cage's music promotes the identification with the here-and-now of reality. But reality in this case is not to be considered in an historical or existential way. In accordance with the principles of his music, Cage rejects historical time and regards time as strictly metrical, a mere succession of moments that do not relate to one another. Identification with the here-and-now presents a category of time beyond history, which excludes all development. Meyer commented on this subject as follows: "To experience reality as it is one must renounce all desires. Man is a part of nature. One must learn to exist like nature, simply existing without purpose." Any dialectical opposition to reality, such as one finds in Schoenberg's 'critical' work, or (in a strictly negative sense) in Webern's work, is rejected by Cage in his ecstatic apology for the immediate experience as the absolute reality. His music is not "an attempt to bring order out of chaos nor to suggest improvements in creation, but simply a way of waking up to the very life we're living, which is so excellent once one gets one's mind and one's desires out of the way and lets it act of its own accord."

With Cage's aleatoricism, the non-dialectical movement in 20th century music reached its peak. This movement is characterized by substituting the concept of process for the concept of the work and by the dissolving of the contradiction between form and content. Ideologically this results in a (utopian) solution of the contradiction between art and reality and in the replacing of historical time by macro-time. The basic ideas of non-dialectical music are similar to those of (American) repetitive music that were outlined earlier. The question that must now be considered is how this non-dialectical movement is to be evaluated, and what the ideological relevance of repetitive music is.

3 Ideology

The development of 20th century music is characterized by the decline of the concept of the work-as-object. The absence of musical content can be evaluated in several ways. Adorno's Marxist analysis leads him to consider the absence of musical content as a form of alienation, and the decay of the subject in and by capitalism is seen as a sign of defeat and regression. Diametrically opposed to this dialectical evolution is the analysis of Gilles Deleuze and Jean-François Lyotard, representatives of a recent development in French thought, usually called *libidinal philosophy*. For these philosophers, the anti-dialectic tendency in 20th century music is a liberation from everyday reality. Gilles Deleuze, in his most important work *Difference and Repetition*, develops a form of logic that breaks away from dialectical thinking, by replacing identity and contradiction with difference and repetition. Deleuze's logical system has a political background which is openly expressed in the writings of Lyotard, who feels that the universalization of the exchange-value system in modern capitalism does not lead to alienation, as Marx believed, but to the abolition of limitations, and the consequent increase in possibilities of communication. Lyotard agrees with Marcuse's view that in modern capitalism opposition has become useless, since it is immediately absorbed by the system. This brings him to the optimistic conclusion that capitalism will destroy itself from within: through a generalized exchange-value system political economics will become libidinal economics. This utopian attitude, which is the opposite of Marxist dialectics, forms the basis of the musical thinking of John Cage and the American repetitive composers.

T W Adorno

In his *Philosophy of New Music*, Adorno attempts to define the function of art in a late-capitalist society characterized by alienation. In an alienated society, art itself must be alienated. Adorno wrote: "Only out of its own confusion can art deal with a confused society." Paradoxically, art criticizes social alienation by absorbing it. Art refuses reconciliation because as far as general social contradictions are concerned, this reconciliation could only be an illusion. According to Adorno, the artist has an insight into his own alienation through which he can transcend it by elucidating it: "The force of art lies in its restraint and its capacity to detect decay and to incorporate and expose it. Art has taken upon itself all the world's darkness and evil. Its joy is to admit sorrow. Its beauty is to denounce any illusion of beauty." Adorno calls the alienated work of art the *negative dialectics* of alienated art. For Schoenberg, this takes the form of a critique. A work of art expresses the social alienation by destroying the concept of the work. The shattered form of a critical work reflects the loss of unity in society. According to Adorno: "Music is truth in so far as it reflects the negative experience: it deals with real suffering." The contradictions or reality disrupt the enclosed nature the traditional work of art has. Negative dialectics do not lead to a synthesis, because the dialectic has become trapped in the contradiction, hence negative dialectics: a synthesis is no longer possible, only a type of dialectic which remains in the position of contradiction.

Schoenberg, whose work is an expression of this negative dialectic, formulated his *Entkunstlung* project in which art is no longer to be truth, but in which the aesthetic category has been replaced by an ethical one. Whereas the traditional, closed work of art assumes an identity of subject and object and the ultimate synthesis of opposites, the critical work rejects this synthesis, leaving object and subject in contradiction. The contradiction between material and structure in the critical work of art reflects the contradiction between individual and society in late capitalism. Critical work is based on dissonance, a metaphor for the totally alienated subject that has lost contact with social reality. In late-capitalist society the subject is isolated, estranged from reality and from society.

Dissonance is at the same time both an indication of extreme subjectivity and the denial of traditional subjectivity. The subject is confirmed, but only as an isolated and empty entity, which has been expelled by the objective order and thus doomed to a solitary existence. According to Lyotard, "Schoenberg regards the reconciliation of subject and object as a perverted parody, a denial of the subject by the objective order." The critical work cannot unite form and content. Unity is scattered, part and whole are separated. Schoenberg's work artificially separates process and aural result, in so far as the aural result is predetermined by the selection of the 12-tone series, which is all but imperceptible in the work (i.e. in this context it is often impossible to perceive the series aurally). The subject submits itself to a self-selected objective system and becomes excluded. "In the dodecaphonic system the subject determines the music through a rational system, but it also becomes an object of this system." The subject has then to face total domination by the objective order. It does not reject this order, nor does it attempt to establish a different order; it simply affirms itself as the exception, which, of course, rather confirms the order.

Adorno says that Schoenberg's work is trapped in contradictions and therefore represents a negative dialectic. There is no totality and reconciliation can only represent impotence. This negative dialectic reacts against the type of dialectic which leads to a synthesis because this synthesis is seen as an impossible one. But because this negative dialectic views these contradictions as if they can still bring about a synthesis, this resistance is still dialectical. This means that Schoenberg's work cannot escape from the dialectic: he rejects the notion of the work but cannot escape from it. Loss of content reflects alienation and *suffering*. Schoenberg denies the subject while at the same time maintaining it as a tragic category, as a crushed, impossible subject. He denies tonality but retains it, since dissonance without consonance would be meaningless. All these contradictions have to do with the remnants of Schoenberg's bourgeois romantic ideology, to whose destruction by capitalism he is a witness.

Adorno's analysis of the music of Igor Stravinsky is the counter-balance of his essay on Schoenberg and is appropriate to all non-dialectical music. According to Adorno, Stravinsky's music is a non-dialectical music which has been taken out of its historical context. On the one hand, Adorno denounces the separation of form and content as alienation, but on the other hand, he maintains this separation as a criterion of truth. Reconciliation of form and content would be impossible as long as the cause of this separation — social alienation — is allowed to continue. According to the dialectical principle that the composer, in confronting his material metaphorically also confronts society, musical contradictions can only be solved when socio-economical contradictions are solved.

With Cage, the dialectical opposition of form and content disappears. Consequently, the opposition between art and life also disappears and music becomes a means of realizing the identification with the here-and-now. With the disappearance of the dialectical link between form and content, the historical category of the work is also removed, replaced by the absolute reality of the immediate experience. François-Bernard Mâche spoke about "a nostalgia for raw innocence and virginal nature." Cage's denunciation of economic alienation is a metaphysical doctrine of non-activity. History as a whole is blamed as being an infringement of the natural order.

Cage's protestant puritanism makes his dream one of a paradise of innocence, untainted by the tree of knowledge. What began as a subjective protest against alienation ends with a rejection of subjectivity as the source of all evil. Instead of history, *myth* is now proposed as a model. As Clytus Gottwald has said: "According to Cage, once the subject has been silenced, one returns to pure being." And Hans Curjel wrote that "Cage refuses choice. The historical duality of mind and matter, life and art, is dispensed with." So Cage's aesthetic project leads logically to an ethical project, anticipating the end of history: the end of economic expansion and political domination and, consequently, the renunciation of the consumer society. Musical nihilism is accompanied by a politics of social nihilism, which, through the illusory unity of life and art, results in historical indifference.

Only a dialectical position ensures the historical continuity of the musical work. Adorno regarded music as a dialectical confrontation with the progress of time. However, this dialectical position has been discarded by Cage and by Young, Riley, Reich and Glass. Their notion of macro-time reduces development to a mere atomized succession, so that, paradoxically, it becomes inert and immobile. In their time-concept there is no longer a rôle for change. These repetitive composers use the concept of metrical time, which is devoid of content. Steve Reich explicitly referred to Cage when he spoke about strictly metrical time in his processes. About Cage, Herman Sabbe coined the phrase "isolated monads without relation", and Clytus Gottwald said of Reich that he "got round the problem of the articulation of time by denying the existence of time."

The most recent development of new music can be summarized as follows: the general movement against the dialectic has led to the denial of the historical category. Unity of form and content represents the repudiation of the contradictions within the very society that shapes the music that gives up its bond with society. The unity of form and content assumes that the contradiction between subject and object, mind and matter is solved. This solution, however, has an alienating effect because of the absence of synthesis in social reality. Music is thus no longer related to historical-dialectical reality and loses its historical continuity. So it returns to non-Western forms that are then stripped of their historical context and used as mere technical formulae and procedures.

Libidinal philosophy

Libidinal philosophy presents a critical analysis of the negative dialectic, which Adorno adjudged to be characteristic of the critical work of art. Jean-François Lyotard finds the concept of the negative dialectic inadequate and it therefore has to be evaluated critically. One could sum up Lyotard's position as follows: "Don't react by falling back on the outmoded category of the individual subject, but think in terms of a future perspective with a free circulation of energy, freed from rule by commodities".

Lyotard finds that the loss of content in the traditional work is more than compensated for in the new music by an increase in libidinal intensity. He criticizes serial music for the way in which it makes for a generalized devaluation of the sound material and the reduction of everything to relationships. In serial music the concept of alienation no longer refers to the subject, but rather concerns the devaluation of the sound as libidinal intensity. This devaluation of the sound material in serial music corresponds, according to Lyotard, with the domination of exchange-value in neo-capitalism. "The domination of rule by commodity degrades the material, and thus everything is reduced to exchange-value and use-value becomes secondary. Only libidinal intensities can escape being considered as exchange-value." Thus Lyotard reacts against the dialectical thinking of Adorno and Schoenberg (for him their ideas about alienation are not comprehensive enough) and he subscribes to the ideas of Cage, because he works in a non-dialectical manner, has no content and no value system. Cage's music, unlike dialectical music, is no longer a "representation of life" but the immediate genesis of life. It deals with pure libidinal intensities, sounds without finality or purpose, music that has neither surface nor depth and defies all representation or identification. A monadic intensity remains, which does not admit of a linear time-perspective, because traditional development has been replaced by a metamorphosis without end or teleology. "Any hierarchy is legitimate, or none is. What is important is the shift of energy," Lyotard says. The intensities refer to each other in all directions, and there is no definite centre: "Development is comparable to a passage without trace. The intensity exists but has no goal or content. The monadism of the intensity allows no possibility of representation." Thus Cage's music is no longer a product, a work that could be defined in a commodity system, but rather a production of productions: not a representation of intensity but the immediate presence of intensity itself. Lyotard defends pure libidinal thinking and libidinal art: "One hears with one's muscles and one no longer communicates ideas but mimetic signs and movements."

Lyotard sees the economic order with its tendency to control libidinal intensities, as the enemy of this libidinal approach. Extreme bursts of energy are denied and reserves are constructed for; immediate gratification is renounced in favour of work that projects this gratification into an indefinite future. And so labour and the dialectic principle represent the principle of reality.

Lyotard notes a reversed tendency in the present consumer society: reserve and providence are abandoned in favour of affluence and overconsumption. To Lyotard these opposing tendencies undermine the law of exchange-value. He distinguishes between a *political economy*, characterized by scarcity, and a *libidinal economy* of profusion and waste. The all-embracing application of the law of exchange-value in modern capitalism would, according to Lyotard, make the economy shift from the political to the libidinal. "If capitalism disappears, it can only happen through excess, because its energy continuously spills beyond its limits. In contrast to capitalism, Marxism limits, and once this limit has been passed, is no longer able to integrate its own oppositions."

Lyotard concludes that the Marxist doctrine has failed practically because the oppositions on which it bases its doctrines seem to have been diminished in modern capitalism by the omnipresent law of exchange-value. Lyotard says: "On the one hand, capitalism goes beyond all the limits of pre-capitalist institutions, while on the other hand its transforming energy permanently undermines its own boundaries and extends them."

Lyotard therefore calls every critical opposition, such as Adorno's, senseless. "Either you leave the hostile territory and don't waste your time with criticism, or you stay, keeping one foot in and the other out." Thus he refers to the Frankfurt School of Adorno, Horkheimer and Habermas as still stressing alienation and still thinking in terms of the subject. Lyotard thinks that "alienation can be evaluated positively, as a means of destroying capitalism from the inside."

Lyotard's viewpoint is resolutely anti-intellectual: "In the age of the rising libido, being right is not important, laughing and dancing is what matters." Whereas political economy is always a matter of limits and negativity, the libidinal economy stands for the free circulation of energy. Like Cage, Lyotard proposes a programme to abolish economic expansion and political determinism. Representatives of the libidinal movement are called marginals, hippies, shop-lifters, parasites and all consumers whose consumption has no economic countervalue, and should in this way undermine the very notion of value.

Nobody has more thoroughly explored the margins of dialectical logic than Gilles Deleuze in books like *Logique du Sens* and *Différence et Répétition*. Deleuze's central notion is that of *plural perspective*, which seems to apply admirably to recent developments in music history. It is no coincidence that the composer Richard Pinhas, a disciple of the American composers of repetitive music, dedicated his recent album *Rhizosphère* to Deleuze. The sleeve note quotes Deleuze: "It is not enough to introduce a new representation of movement. Representation is still mediation. A movement has to be created in the work itself, that can move the mind without any representation. The movement itself has to become *work* without mediation."

Deleuze, like Lyotard, assumes the failure of representation, but he does not explain it nor does he try to evaluate it, he simply underwrites it. About the work of art, he says: "The main characteristic of the modern work of art is the absence of centre, and of convergence. It is a problematic work and nothing more." The modern work of art is problematic in taking, through this decentralization, the form of a "labyrinth without thread (Ariadne has hung herself)."

Out of Deleuze's critique of dialectical thought a new *problematic logic* is developed. From this logic there emerges the essence of an object that results from its difference from other objects. This is contrary to the dialectical method in which an object only exists through its neutralization of the opposition. For Deleuze the de-centralized work of art is a-dialectical because it replaces the concepts

of *identity* and *opposition* with those of *distinction* and *repetition*. It is
not a question of "reducing opposites to a single identity but of
affirming their distance as that which relates one to the other as being
different", he says. So instead of opposition Deleuze sees a process in
which two objects are defined by their difference and are subjected to
simultaneous affirmation which in itself affirms their difference.
Thus repetition becomes an affirmation of difference.

Furthermore, Deleuze replaces the identity by that of the *field*: "a
complex conglomerate of phenomena that are no longer reduceable to
one common denominator", as he calls it. Because the decentralized
work does not have a teleological development, Deleuze speaks of a
monadic distribution: the singular intensities are in a process that is
ever changing and shifting, generating itself at each moment. This
intensity has no content other than itself: "Each intensity wants to be
itself, to be its own goal and repeats and imitates itself." Thus, along
with dialectics, the hierarchy of work has been removed. Essential for
the dialectic work is the distinction between model (essence) and its
imitation (the phenomenon), which are hierarchically linked. This
hierarchy is based on the identity of both, and thus on their similarity.
In the decentralized work, the model disappears, and the dialectical
concept of identity is replaced by that of repetition, and there no longer
exists a hierarchy in the work. Deleuze conceives the phenomenon
(imitation) as separate from the essence (the model) and refers to a
simulation (simulacre): a phenomenon that does not represent anything anymore and has no content other than itself as pure intensity.
"The real subject of repetition is the simulation that is no longer
representation." (Lyotard uses, in this context, the term *'figure'*).

These *simulations* or *figures* are pre-individual and as a result the
work is a-subjective and anonymous. Repetition in the decentralized
work differs from that in a dialectical work, because it is not static but
differentiating: it is not repetition of the same but of the same as
something else. Jacques Derrida speaks about "an art without economy, without reserve and without history". Instead of representation
that is a reproduction of something that existed before, there is
merely presentation: "Pure presence, no reproduction, without inner
difference or duality". Derrida refers to unities which are outside
time, that is, take place in a non-time and are nothing short of pure
intensity.

Dialectics and the libido

In *Das Unbewußte* (The Unconscious), Sigmund Freud defined unconscious libidinal processes and characterized them by the lack of awareness of contradiction, by mobility, timelessness and by the substitution of psychic contents for external realities. Freud noted the absence of negation, doubt and contradiction in the unconscious system. "The unconscious system is not governed by laws of logic, especially not by the law of contradiction. Contradictory tendencies can exist side by side." In the unconscious system, energy is mobile and flows freely. It is not determined by a causal teleology but extends freely over the whole field of representations, resulting in a high degree of mobility. Because no negativity exists in the unconscious, there is no dialectical time. "Unconscious processes are timeless, that is, they are not structured in time, do not change with time and are in no way related to time." The timelessness of the unconscious process is also due to its weak relationship with reality. According to Freud, "The unconscious takes no notice of reality. The pleasure principle prevails and everything depends on the strength of the impulse and its relation to the principles of pleasure and reality." The unconscious "substitutes psychic realities for external realities."

These characteristics of the unconscious process, listed by Freud, are similar to Deleuze's description of the art work without centre. It is therefore no coincidence that the non-dialectical thinking of Lyotard is often referred to as 'libidinal philosophy'. Deleuze discards the idea of representation and replaces it by immediate, actual intensity. Representation is always reproduction, whereas the thing itself is *pure presence, without reproduction, without internal difference or duality*, according to Jacques Derrida. And because there is no economy or reserve of intensity, there is no historical category, since intensity is totally outside time (Derrida uses the term *non-time*, which is the self-representation of intensity itself). This libidinal dimension has only recently been recognized, yet it was already implicit in Cage's insistence on the autonomy of sound and it was ideologically reflected in the denial of history. We maintain that this libidinal context has been recognized explicitly only by these American composers of repetitive music. In a musical context this libidinal content expresses itself in an American music that is characterized by repetition and a process which can be recognised immediately by the listener. The process shifts the listener's attention from the content of change to the mobile game of change itself. In repetitive music this change is a kind of new content, and in a way one gets the suggestion of an entirely free flow of energy.

It is somewhat less easy to define the function of repetition in repetitive music. Freud distinguished between repetition in the service of *Eros*, the pleasure principle (die Sexualtriebe), and repetition in the service of *Thanatos*, the death instinct (die Totestriebe). In Freudian thinking Eros stands for the ego, representation and control of intensity. According to Freud, repetition serving Eros is *Bemächtigungstrieb* (the desire to control) whereas reproduction is pleasurable because it is a manifestation of control. To Freud, the principle of the constant is the basis of the pleasure principle. The ego strives towards internal stability by reducing libidinal energy. Hence repetition in the service of Eros is repetition of identical elements and is therefore reproduction. This is opposed to repetition in the service of the death instinct; to Freud, Thanatos is a conglomerate of the libidinal energy that is a permanent threat to the integrity of the ego.

In repetitive music, repetition in the service of the death instinct prevails. Repetition is not repetition of identical elements, so it is not reproduction, but the repetition of the identical in another guise. The processes of repetitive music are impersonal and this anonimity is enhanced by repetition, continuing until it can no longer be recognized and, in the end, must turn against the ego. As has already been pointed out, repetition in repetitive music is technically identical to repetition in traditional music. The only difference is the context in which it is used. In traditional music, repetition is a device for creating recognisability, reproduction for the sake of the representing ego. In repetitive music, repetition does not refer to eros and to the ego, but to the libido and to the death instinct. Process and repetition produce a shift from the dialectical principle of reality onto the unconscious level, where external realities are replaced by psychic ones.

The ecstatic state induced by this music, which could also be called *a state of innocence, an hypnotic state,* or *a religious state*, is created by an independent libido, freed of all the restrictions of reality. Repetitive music only appears to succeed when the listener consciously discards his dialectical way of listening. Ecstasy in other words can only occur when the ego can let go.

Repetitive music can lead to psychological regression. The so-called *religious* experience of repetitive music is in fact a camouflaged erotic experience. One can speak of a controlled pseudo-satisfaction because the abandoning of dialectical time does not really happen but is only imaginary. The libido, freed from the external world, turns towards the ego to obtain imaginary satisfaction. Freud defined this as a regression and a "return to the infantile experience of hallucinatory satisfaction".

To what extent the ecstatic dimension is consciously pursued and to what extent it may even be the main purpose of composing repetitive music, is not clear. It is certainly one of the main reasons for its popularity. The drug-like experience and the imaginary satisfaction it brings about are even more obvious in disco music and space-rock, the popular derivatives of repetitive music. This music at least leaves no room for doubt about its intentions. The same criticism of imaginary satisfaction can be equally applied to the whole of the non-dialectical movement. Processes of production without negativity are utopian and historically unrealistic, like the absolute libido in repetitive music.

But one must consider the possibility that the current non-dialectical movement in music and philosophy could be searching for something quite different from the liberation it claims. Libidinal philosophy suits the one-dimensional society as described by Marcuse. He says that late-capitalist society has an extraordinary capacity to turn emancipatory movements into movements that accommodate the ruling monopolist powers. "The breaking down of the ego-functions are intended to create and increase control and to strengthen the institutional monopolist powers."

According to Marcuse, the breakdown of dialectics is not a solution but is a symptom of the disease — the desertion from history in favour of a utopian world. This can only bring pseudo-satisfaction and will probably serve to strengthen the historical impasse for the worse.

Bibliography

Part 1

BURDE, W., *Rundfunk Manuscript*, Berlin, 1974.

CAUX, D., *Sur La Monte Young*, in *Art Vivant*, 30, 1972.

LA MONTE YOUNG, *Selected Writings. Interview with R. Kostelanez and H. Friedrick*, Munich, 1969.

LENTIN, J.-P., *Interview with Phil Glass*, in *Le Monde de la Musique*, Paris, Editions Le Monde et Télérama, 1978.

NYMAN, M., *Experimental Music, Cage and Beyond*, New York, Schirmer Books, 1974.

NYMAN, M., *Tim Souster's Night at the Proms*, in *Tempo*, 94, 1970.

REICH, S., *Writings about Music*, New York, Universal Editions, The Press of the Nova Scola College of Art and Design, Halifax Canada and University Press, 1974.

REICH, S., Text *Music for Mallet Instruments, Voices and Organ*, D.G.G. 27410106.

RILEY, T., Text *A Rainbow in Curved Air*, CBS S 3461180.

SABBE, H., *Stroop uit de Kosmos*, in *Kunst en Kultuur*, 1, Brussels, 1979.

SCHNEBEL, D., *Tendenzen in der neuen Amerikanischen Musik*, in *Avant-garde, Jazz, Pop, Tendenzen Zwischen Tonalität und Atonalität*, Mainz-London, Schott, 1978.

STIEBLER, E., *Ueberlegungen zur periodischen Musik*, in *Avant-Garde, Jazz, Pop, Tendenzen Zwischen Tonalität und Atonalität*, Mainz-London, Schott, 1978.

STOIANOVA, I., *Musique Répétitive*, in *Musique en Jeu*, Paris, Seuil, 1977, pp. 64-74.

Part 2

ADORNO, T.W., *Philosophie der neuen Musik*, Frankfurt/Main, Ullstein Bücher, 1958.

BOULEZ, P., *Possibilités*, in *Revue Musicale*, Paris, 1952.

CAGE, J., *A year from Monday*, London, Wesleyan University Press, 1968.

LYOTARD, J.-F., *Des Dispositifs Pulsionnels*, Paris, Union Générale des Editions, Série 10/18, 1973.

MANN, T., *Doktor Faustus*, Frankfurt/Main, Fischer Taschenbuch Verlag, 1975.

MEYER, L.B., *Music, the Arts and Ideas*, Chicago Press, 1967.

NYMAN, M., *Experimental Music, Cage and Beyond*, New York, Schirmer Books, 1974.

POUSSEUR, A., *Vers un nouvel Univers Sonore*, in *Esprit*, Paris, 1960.

SCHNEBEL, D., *Denkbare Musik*, Keulen, Du Mont-Schauberg, 1972.

STOCKHAUSEN, K., *Texte I: Neue Zusammenhänge zwischen Aufführungsdauer, Werkdauer und Moment*, Keulen, Du Mont-Schauberg, 1959.

STOCKHAUSEN, K., *Wie die Zeit vergeht*, in *Die Reihe*, 3, Keulen, Du Mont-Schauberg, 1959.

Part 3

ADORNO, T.W., *Vers une musique informelle*, in *Quasi una Fantasia, Musikalische Schriften II*. Frankfurt/Main, 1957.

AURON, D., *L'appareil musical*, Paris, Union Générale des Editions, Série 10/18, 1978.

CAGE, J., *A Year from Monday*, London, Wesleyan University Press, 1968.

CURJEL, H., *John Cage*, in *Melos*, 9, 1955.

DELEUZE, G., *Logique du Sens*, Paris, Union Générale des Editions, Série 10/18, 1969.

DELEUZE, D., Text R. *Pinhas 'Rhizosphère'*, Cobra COB 37005 12.

DERRIDA, J., *L'écriture et la Différence*, Paris, Collection Tel Quel, Editions du Seuil, 1969.

FREUD, S., *Works X: The Unconscious*, London, Imago Ltd.

GOTTWALD, C., *Fragments d'une analyse de Songbooks de Cage*, in *La Musique en Projet*, Paris, Collection Cahiers Renaud-Barrault, Gallimard, IRCAM, 1975.

HAMEL, P.-M., *Through music to the self*, Tisbury-Wiltshire, 1978.

LYOTARD, J.-F., *Des Dispositifs Pulsionnels*, Paris, Union Générale des Editions, Série 10/18, 1973.

LYOTARD, J.-F., and AARON, D., *A few words to sing,* in *Musique en Jeu,* 2, Paris, Editions du Seuil, 1971.

MARCUSE, H., *The One-Dimensional Man,* Neuered, 1960.

MACHE, F. B., *A propos de Cage,* in *Musique en Jeu,* 2, Paris, Editions du Seuil, 1971.

SABBE, H., *Philosophie de la musique la plus récente, essai d'extrapolation à partir de la Philosophie de la Nouvelle Musique d'Adorno,* in *Musique en Jeu,* 7, Paris, Seuil, 1972.

SMALL, C., *Music-Society-Education,* London, John Calder, 1977.

ACKNOWLEDGMENTS

Copyright Robert Adler: ex 3
Copyright La Monte Young: exs 4, 5, 6, 7, 8
Copyright Terry Riley: exs 9, 10, 11, 12, 13, p43
Copyright Universal Edition (London): exs 1, 15, 16, 17, 18, 21, 22, 24
Copyright Steve Reich: exs 19, 20, 23, 25, 26
Copyright C Mercereau: ex 27
Copyright Philip Glass: exs 28, 29, 30, 31, 32, 33, 34, 35, 36, 37, 38, 39, 40
                                    endpapers: extracts from *Music in Contrary Motion*

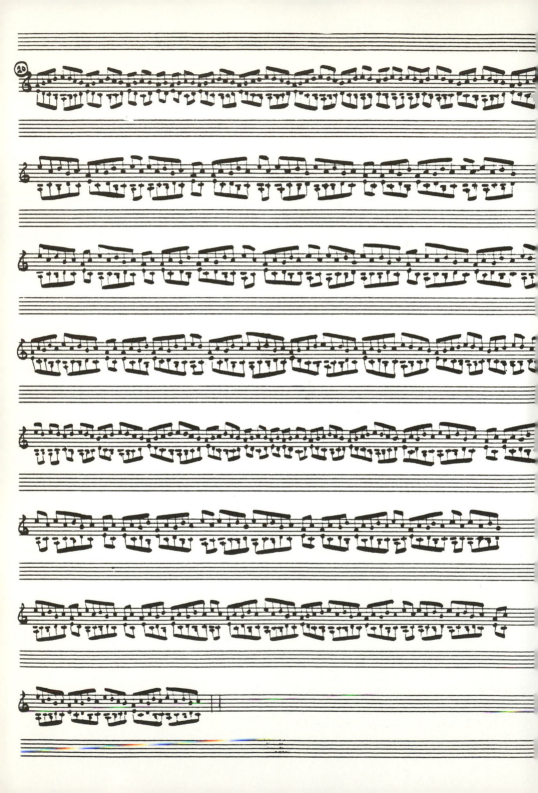

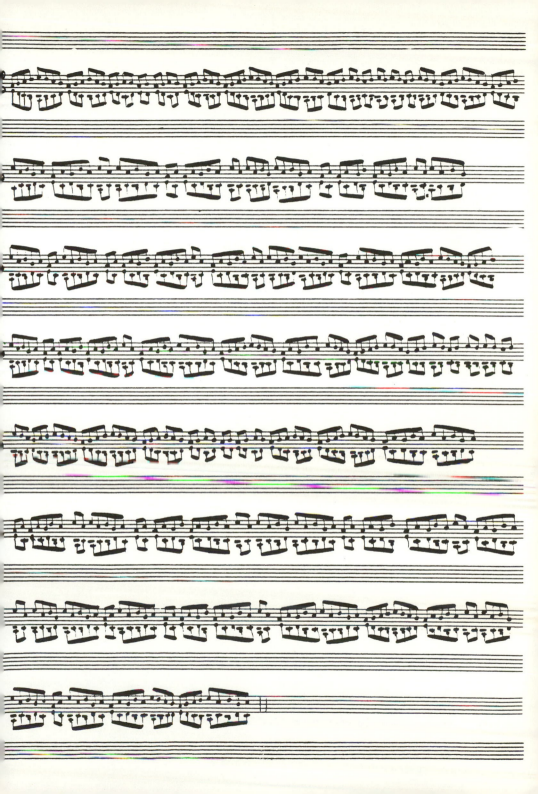